JUST ADD SALT

A Single Mother's Quest
to Save Her Daughter's Life
and Feed Her Soul

LEAH MILANA BAUER

To my daughter, Grace-Rose:
Thank you for teaching me how to be a mom. I love you.

To my mother, Grace:
Same.

In 1965, after hearing his mother make phone calls
to raise money for Cystic Fibrosis research, the four-year-old
told her it sounded like she was working for "sixty-five roses."

Since then, the term has been used widely throughout
the CF community and to help kids with the disease pronounce it.

It's the reason for the roses…and pure coincidence
in Grace-Rose's name.

CONTENTS

FOREWORD

I first met Leah sixteen years ago at the gym. I was wearing a Cystic Fibrosis t-shirt, she walked right up, struck up a conversation, and told me her five-year-old daughter, Grace-Rose, had CF. I told her my eight-year-old niece had it as well, and we immediately connected. There's something comforting in finding someone who understands so deeply at least one aspect of your life. To this day, and even more so all those years ago, so few people know about Cystic Fibrosis.

Over time, I got more involved in their efforts to raise awareness and funds for CF, and I found myself inspired not only by their dedication but the way they both carried the weight of it all with so much strength and grace. A shared love of the theater and sushi between Grace-Rose and I only made it feel more like being with family. I have an immense amount of pride being an advocate for their foundation.

One of the things that stands out in Leah's story is her love for food and cooking. Growing up, meals were a way for her family to spend quality time together. But for families living with CF, food is complicated. It's not just about enjoying a meal together—it's about battling nutrition issues, trying to gain weight, and managing a disease that makes something as simple as eating feel like a challenge. Each chapter ends with a recipe, a small reflection of how food is woven into the fabric of her life, both as a joy and as a hurdle.

In a world often defined by hardship and resilience, Leah stands as a beacon of strength and hope. Her memoir is not just a recounting of extraordinary experiences, it's a heartfelt testament to the complexities of love, loss, and the unyielding spirit of a mother. Leah's journey is raw, emotional, and real. As a single mother navigating the challenges of raising a daughter with a life-threatening illness, she invites us into a journey that is both heartbreaking and uplifting, filled with moments that will shatter your heart yet inspire your soul.

Each page resonates with the mother's battle cry; raw, powerful, and undeniably human. It's about using everything you have, whether that's strength, love, or food, to keep going. Leah shares her story with an authenticity that compels us to rally behind her and Grace-Rose. Their unwavering determination to fight for life, despite seemingly insurmountable odds, is a call to arms for all who believe in the beauty of survival and the transformative power of love.

This memoir will stay with you long after you finish it. You'll find yourself embracing not only her journey but the joy that brings people together, even when life's challenges feel overwhelming. You'll be inspired, as I've been from the first moment I met them, to fight for the things that matter most — and maybe even try some of her recipes along the way.

– JR Bourne

INTRODUCTION

People with Cystic Fibrosis lose four times more salt than those without CF because their sweat glands can't reabsorb sweat back into the blood. The faulty CFTR gene controls the movement of chloride and water in and out of the cells.

This is a story about fear, friendship, faith, and food…

As a new mother, I was told that I must take care of myself first in order to take the best care of my child. At the rate that life was happening, and new medical information was being delivered to me, I never had this luxury…or at least I was unaware of how to realize it. They say to secure your own oxygen mask before helping your child with theirs, but what if only one mask drops?

In the pages that follow, you will read about my twenty-one-year journey of raising a daughter alone and helping her navigate the tumultuous ride that is Cystic Fibrosis (CF). It is one of the first books to shed light on a largely unchartered territory in the CF community: adulthood. Thanks to research and medicine, Grace-Rose (or as I often call her, "GR") is leading a life that was unimaginable when she was born. It also explores the relationship between mother and daughter as both discover an independence they never thought possible.

Every book about Cystic Fibrosis from a parent's perspective that I was ever given focused on loss and grief. I wanted this one to be about living and hope!

There have been countless challenges along the way, but just as many blessings. Living life with a sense of urgency, seeing its fragilities, witnessing its miracles, learning empathy, and discovering altruism are just a few of the things GR has taught me.

Family, food, and conversation were pillars of my upbringing and significant in how I raised my child. Sharing meals created a strong connection, allowing us to easily and openly communicate.

Growing up, family dinners were sacred, sometimes lasting as long as two hours! When the phone rang (one landline, no answering machine) someone would be allowed to answer it only to say we could not be interrupted during family dinner. The caller was welcome to try back later, but by then it would often be too late to talk, or we still had too much homework to finish before bedtime.

I recall my mother coming home after a full day of work at her own office and preparing a four or five-course meal. We all had to participate in some way – helping with prep, setting the table, clearing the table, or doing the dishes. Prep time was a coveted task because it meant conversation time alone with Mom.

The dinner itself was also a time of lively discussion. Both my parents were avid readers and curious about the world – particularly when it came to education, travel, and art – and they shared these passions with me and my siblings. My dad would often print out topics about world events, politics, or sports and leave them on our plates as discussion prompts. My little sister Kate was very young, so after about an hour our six-top would often turn into a five-top. Tired of the discussion, she would try to entertain us by running around the table with a flower pot on her head or some other attention-grabbing routine. She would continue until she was exhausted enough to fall asleep somewhere around or underneath the table. We had no TV growing up so that was never a distraction. Those one- to two-hour nightly dinners were a way of ensuring we stayed in communication and connected. It strengthened our bond.

In high school, a civics teacher asked for a show of hands to indicate how many parents were still together. I was one of only a few hands that went up. He then asked how many families still had dinner together and I was the only one to raise my hand. That surprised me. To this day, I think we can all appreciate the value of mealtime and how it represents community, conversations, learning, and sharing. In fact, in high school, I, along with my best friend Rebecca, started hosting monthly dinner parties on my balcony – a ritual everyone enjoyed.

Later, food would become an ongoing source of conflict between me and Grace-Rose's medical team. Food, salt, hydration, and nutrition were constant topics of discussion at the CF clinic. Her team insisted on placing a feeding tube in her stomach; I spent years trying to fight it.

This is why I have chosen to end each chapter with a dish that relates to our story. The recipes are primarily from the three cities where we spent the most time over the past twenty-one years: Los Angeles, New Orleans, and New York. Some are from chefs and adapted by restaurants, others are homegrown. Hopefully, they will inspire group dinners and conversation while imprinting lasting memories that feed your soul.

ONE

SALT TEST - DIAGNOSIS

I asked my mom to meet me on Aline, the side street to the hospital, in twenty minutes. I needed enough time to throw my tattered Holy Cross Basketball sweatshirt over my hospital gown and convince the nurses that I was going up to the fifth-floor chapel to pray. I was not to be disturbed until I returned to my room. Without question, my mom was waiting for me outside. She knew where we were headed.

As we drove down Magazine Street, I gazed out of the window, staring at the trees. I vividly recall the bright green leaves swaying slowly as the sunlight streamed through. Everything looked brighter, multidimensional. It's hard to explain, but it was as though my life was about to enter an entirely different realm of reality.

And it was...

We pulled up to the Children's Hospital to find my father already waiting for us.

"Have you seen the doctor?" I asked anxiously, "Heard anything?"

He shook his head. "Not yet, they've been in surgery for about an hour."

As soon as I found out that my newborn would have to undergo surgery to remove the meconium ileus blocking her intestines, I knew I was going to be there. GR had been born in an adult hospital via emergency C-section, then whisked away and rushed to Children's Hospital. Aside from the brief moment when she was placed on my chest, followed by a hand-held goodbye from her tiny incubator, I was not able to see or be with my baby.

This was completely unfathomable to me, given my pleasant and relatively easy pregnancy. I had stayed active, swimming laps in the summer and taking long walks around Audubon Park. I worked for myself and had continued to do so. I enjoyed feeling the movement in my belly whenever Eli, her father, put on salsa music. We had decided to be surprised about the sex of the baby and decorated the small room in our Magazine Street apartment with various artworks rather than the usual pink or blue. I had taken Bradley Method classes and was fully prepared to have a natural childbirth, along with music and candles.

Everything changed the day before Thanksgiving when I went for my thirty-ninth-week doctor's appointment. It was fairly routine, until he began to listen for the heartbeat, which he discovered was higher than usual. He wanted me to go across the street to get one last ultrasound to make sure the baby wasn't breech.

As I walked across the street and entered the room where I was to get my ultrasound, the nurse was not there. Instead, a man sat at the computer and said he could do it. I told him that I would wait for the nurse. When she did arrive, she said, "He's our neonatal specialist and may be here for a while. You should just let him do it." So, I did.

A few minutes into the process of the wand circulating my stomach, he asked, "What's the ethnicity of your husband?"

I stared at him in utter confusion. How was that even relevant? What was he seeing?

"Well, I'm not married but he is Afro-Cuban. Why?"

He told me he was "taking measurements," and I glanced at the nurse to see the same confused look on her face. I just wanted to know if my baby was breech or not so I could go home.

He left for a moment, then returned with a phone in his hand. "Your doctor is on the line," he said, as he passed me the phone. My doctor then said,

"Leah, call your family. You're having this baby right now. We need to do an emergency C-section."

"Wait, what is going on?" I asked.

He explained that while measuring the baby's abdomen the technician had discovered it was severely distended. This was urgent. If we waited it could cause serious harm to the baby, as well as to me if I tried to have it naturally.

My mom and Eli met me at the hospital. My father was about to leave for Massachusetts, where my grandmother was in hospice, but he stopped in for a quick visit and to offer me support. Keep me posted, he told us.

As they wheeled me into the anesthesiologist, my heart began to race, not just because of the nerves of receiving this shot, but I also recognized the anesthesiologist. He played for the team we had just beaten in the playoffs. With a massive needle about to pierce my backside, all I could do was hope he didn't recognize me too!

Moments later, they made the incision in my stomach, and after what felt like a little bit of a tug-of-war with my belly, my baby appeared.

I was certain I was having a boy and had already picked out his name, so I hadn't thought much about girls' names. Regardless, I wanted it to be a surprise - and it certainly was!

When they announced that it was a girl, I looked at Eli and without hesitation said, "Grace."

Grace is my mom's name. She'd also been named after her grandmother, Grace, who I adored as a young girl.

We affectionately refer to them as "The Real OG's" or "Original Grace's."

Eli nodded, then said his own mom's name – Rose.

I thought for a minute, Grace-Rose... a double first name, I liked the sound of it.

She was born the day before Thanksgiving and her surgery was scheduled for the day after. I sat in the hospital with my mom and Eli eating ice chips on Thanksgiving Day. I was still recovering from the C-section and hadn't been discharged yet. I was not going to miss my baby's first surgery. They were about to cut her stomach open just as they had mine and I didn't want her to have to undergo that alone. Five draining hours later, the doctor stepped out. He looked a little surprised to see me with a sweatshirt covering my hospital gown, but he didn't comment on my obvious escape from the hospital.

He told us that Grace-Rose was in recovery and would be in the NICU for a while. They had to cut out part of her tiny intestines to clear the blockage. Later, I would notice she had the same incision on her stomach as I did. In years to come, we would bond over our matching "smiley face" scars.

The surgeon continued to describe the meconium ileus, a bowel obstruction that occurs in newborns when the meconium, the first stool passed after birth, becomes thick and sticky and blocks the small intestine (ileum). He then said those words I would never forget: "When babies present with meconium ileus there's a ninety percent chance they have Cystic Fibrosis. Let's just pray Grace-Rose falls into the other ten percent."

Shaken by the news, I returned to the hospital and snuck back into my room. When the nurse came in, I told her I needed to be discharged right away. She told me that it was too soon and I wasn't ready. I politely but firmly let her know that either way, I'd be leaving. What she didn't know was that I already had. The head doctor understood my angst and said she'd allow me to leave, but if there were any complications (they would give me a list of things to look out for) I had to return immediately. Also, she wanted me to rest and not push too hard.

I left that afternoon. The following morning, I started what would become my routine four-mile walk to and from the hospital.

As my two-week-old lay in a small incubator, her entire body wrapped in gauze with heat lamps meant to make her sweat, I couldn't help but wonder what the outcome of this test would determine.

I sat staring, watching her face redden, her eyes locking on mine as if she was expecting an explanation, not understanding why they would purposely put her in so much discomfort.

It's known as a sweat test. It measures the amount of chloride in sweat.

Babies born with Cystic Fibrosis have two to five times the normal amount of chloride in their sweat. In a sweat test, the skin is stimulated to produce enough sweat to be absorbed into a special collector and then analyzed.

A NICU nurse walked by and took note of the situation, then looked at me. "Oh dear," she said, "Just pray it's not CF. Those babies don't live very long." As if that wasn't enough, she added, "I used to work on the CF floor at the Hospital, but it was too depressing to stay.

Their average lifespan is about ten years."

I let that sink in.

When I returned home that evening, since we were not allowed to spend the night in the hospital, I looked up CF online, and what I saw terrified me.

Cystic Fibrosis is a progressive, genetic disease that affects the lungs, pancreas, sinuses, and other organs. It is life-threatening with no known cure. The average life expectancy is mid-teens.

While this was going on, Eli was out entertaining his mother, also known as *Abuela* (the Spanish word for grandmother.) Abuela, who lived in New York, had come down to New Orleans for the first time to see her new grandchild.

The fact that our daughter was not home with us and potentially had a life-threatening disease didn't seem to affect him. I think he believed that whatever it was, it could be "prayed away." This was probably the first time I realized just how alone I was going to be on this journey.

Every morning, I would go to the hospital to sit with Grace-Rose. Throughout the day, I would hold her, slightly intimidated by all the connecting chords. I would talk to her, ask the nurses questions, watch her vitals, and help feed her.

I had been pumping breast milk since she was born, even though the nurses told me it would be a lost cause. They said she'd never latch on once she'd been given a bottle or alternate methods of nutrition. I insisted. I would bring my milk to the NICU each morning and watch as they added it to her medicine and formula. Knowing the benefits of breastfeeding, this felt like something I could do, in an otherwise helpless situation. It was that intangible connection, the one thing I actually had control over.

My insistence resulted in several bouts of mastitis, as it's abnormal for a new mother to rely solely on pumping for an entire month. Mastitis is when your breast becomes swollen, hot, painful, and can feel like a hardened rock. It can cause nipple discharge and bleeding from cracked nipples. It often results from pumping too much, as was my case, or not removing equal amounts of milk. It can also cause flu-like symptoms, chills, tiredness, and fever. At one point, my fever was high enough that I wasn't allowed into the NICU, causing me more anguish than the actual pain. However painful it was, I was willing to continue for the sheer fact that my child was suffering too.

After a week of showing up with reddened eyes from sleepless nights, constant crying, and endless worry, I realized the effect this must be having on my baby. I thought to myself, *I can't bring this energy in here, why would she want to come home to this?*

I was, in fact, grieving a life not yet lived.

I began taking longer walks en route to the hospital each morning in order to meditate and work out any sadness or fears that I had. I needed to arrive as a more positive, higher-vibrational mother. I was determined to get Grace-Rose home for Christmas.

It had been two weeks. I still wasn't eating or sleeping. I was crying so much at night that Eli would ask me to stay in another room. I was confused and afraid. I had wonderful friends who would stop by and simply leave bags of fruit, nuts, and granola bars to encourage me to eat. They would aslo leave notes with these gifts that read, "You need to eat for your baby's nutrients," along with prayers and other sweet messages. Emails were the most common form of communication at the time, and when I couldn't respond to the influx my mom would print the notes so I could read them at the hospital. It was a thoughtful distraction.

Note: when someone you know is going through something difficult and you're unsure whether to send a message, do it, even if you don't know it will be read. It likely will be, and it can help.

We had to wait two long weeks before they could perform the sweat test. Apparently, this was how long it would take to get her to produce sweat. The doctor finally came in with the results. I was sitting next to Eli, who showed up only to find out the test results with me. That's when I heard the familiar voice of "Doc," from our Championship basketball team at the Jewish Community Center. I'd obviously known he was a doctor but had no idea he was the pulmonary specialist at Children's Hospital.

We sat in front of Grace-Rose, watching them carefully remove all the gauze. It wasn't until we turned around that Doc recognized us, and the minute I saw his expression, I knew.

"Oh, Leah," he said, "I am so sorry. The test came back positive."

At that moment it felt like my world was in fragments. I also knew I had no choice but to keep it together.

The discharge papers came through on December 23rd. We'd have to spend one full night in a hospital room alone with Grace-Rose for observation and in the event of any emergency. Just as I had promised her, she'd be home for Christmas. My Thanksgiving baby and my Christmas gift.

The day they were discharging Grace-Rose they asked if I'd like to try to put her on my breast. I watched as they slowly detached the connecting chords one by one, then she was lifted out of her tiny NICU bed and handed to me. They set up an area with a folding screen for privacy and as soon as I held her to my chest, she latched on. I had been so concerned that I had forever lost that initial bonding moment, as I had been told I would. This was her way of letting me know I hadn't.

Relieved, I thought, *I'm not going to let her go, at least, not until she's ready.* It would take two and a half years to wean her off.

It was the first time Grace-Rose beat the odds, but it wouldn't be the last.

That Christmas turned out to be bittersweet. We spent Christmas Eve at my parents' home, so happy that GR was out of the hospital, only to find out the following morning that my grandmother had passed away. I watched everyone scrambling to make flight arrangements, knowing my baby and I couldn't go with them. Still, I couldn't help but sense that this was Grammy's way of passing on her "fighting spirit."

She had held out until we were home. A year and a half later, I would take GR to the tennis courts in Scituate, Massachusetts that were dedicated to Grammy and share that energy.

When I was pregnant, I had learned some things about Eli that were deeply troubling. Basically, he was a compulsive liar, unable to communicate about it, and clearly had no intention to change or take accountability. After months of torment, I had come to the conclusion that it was best for us to separate. He wanted to be part of our lives and I wanted him to be as well. I just knew it wouldn't be in a committed relationship. I had known him for ten years, and we had been close friends long before we were partners. This was how all my meaningful long-term relationships had started, and I took pride in the fact that I was still friends with my exes (and still am to this day.) I knew it was going to be difficult because I would have to figure out a living situation on my own, with a newborn, and a newly diagnosed life-threatening disease. In the meantime, I had to focus every ounce of energy on GR's very strict regimen.

The first few months consisted of me organizing all her medicines and feeds. She had jaundice, so they were keeping a close eye on her liver. I was prescribed ursodiol for this, which meant I had to use a tiny syringe to put the directed amount into the milk that I had pumped and filled with additional formula for the added calories. Otherwise, the doctor said, if I didn't add formula, she wouldn't get enough nutrients to thrive.

I was extremely careful when it came to this dosage, as the doctors had warned me that too little and she could have liver failure, too much and she could die. I had a chart on the wall with everything that needed to be administered, in which dose and at what time. Also, before she could eat or drink anything, I needed to get her to take the prescribed digestive enzymes, which she couldn't produce on her own due to her pancreatic insufficiency, in order for her to absorb the nutrients from the food.

Since she wasn't able to swallow the pills, I had to open them and pour the little pellets inside the pill into a small mixture of oatmeal with water. I would then quickly, before they could dissolve and become useless, have to stick it on my finger and massage it down her throat.

Every other day, a home health nurse came to check her weight and vitals. They wanted her to eat every two hours. My days and nights were filled with the oatmeal and enzyme combo, formula feeding by bottle, some at specific times with medicine, boiling and cleaning the bottles, then breastfeeding and pumping the rest. It was all-consuming. The most we could do was take small walks, usually to my favorite nearby coffee shop. I've always thought that the discharge of a new mom should come with a complimentary coffee card.

GR slept in the bed between me and Eli, on a pillow propped up to help her breathe. I set alarms for every two hours to wake her from a peaceful sleep and feed her. Oatmeal with enzymes, bottle formula, breastfeed. I would do this until she fell back asleep on my breast and then sneak into the kitchen to finish pumping, boiling bottles, and getting medicine and formula ready for the next feed.

Our kitchen had now started to resemble a science lab. One evening as I was boiling bottles, I drifted off to sleep right on the kitchen table.

I was jolted awake by the smell of smoke and rising flames. I had set the kitchen on fire. Apparently, the bottles had boiled all the way down and melted the pot. Eli raced into the kitchen and I rushed GR out of the house in fear of what the smoke might do to her fragile lungs.

I wrapped her in blankets and we spent the rest of the night in the car to avoid any inhalation.

I was so caught up in the magnitude of this responsibility; I had no idea that sleep deprivation was a real, dangerous thing.

Gumbo

Modified from Kit Wohl's *New Orleans Classic Gumbos & Soups* featuring Chef Donald Link's recipe for Black-Eyed Peas and Pork Gumbo. Chef Link donated food to our initial GR4CF events. Gumbo is the official cuisine of Louisiana, its origin from a variety of cultures. Just like GR.

Ingredients:

1 1/2 c. flour

1 1/2 c. oil

2 c. diced onion

1 c. diced green pepper

1 c. diced celery

3 T. chopped garlic

1 1/2 gal. pork or chicken stock

1 1/2 lbs. okra sliced crosswise 1/2 inch wide and seared in lard until lightly browned

2 c. cooked black-eyed peas (cook in chicken stock with large pieces of mirepoix that can be removed after cooking)

2 c. bacon braised greens (collards or mustards cooked in bacon and onions with sugar, vinegar, hot sauce and salt and pepper)

2-3 lbs. pork butt (raw weight) fully smoked and chopped

2 T. Filé

1 T. Thyme

1 T. Chile powder

1 T. White pepper

1 T. Paprika

2 T. Black pepper

1 T. Cayenne pepper

3 each bay leaves

Method:

Make a dark roux using the oil and flour. (Paul Prudhomme's *Louisiana Kitchen* has some good roux techniques, advice, and gumbo recipes).

As soon as roux is the right color (just past red and turning back to brown but not scorched or smelling really burnt) add the diced vegetables and garlic.

Add the stock and stir very frequently to bring up to a simmer. Simmer for about 1 hour, stirring lots. Skim all the fat that separates out.

Taste the gumbo. It should not taste pasty and like the roux anymore. If it does you may need to add more stock up to 1/2 gallon. This is different every time depending on the exact measurement of flour, strength of starch in the flour, and degree of cooking of the roux, among other things, so add the stock in stages and let it cook and come together before adding more.

When the gumbo is the right consistency add the okra, black-eyed peas, greens, pork, and seasoning. Allow to return to a simmer and adjust the seasoning.

Serve with steamed rice (traditional) or potato salad (Cajun-style)

Another favorite gumbo is from the late Leah Chase of Dooky Chase's restaurant in New Orleans. Hers is a more traditional seafood and sausage style.

Of a roux, she said, "The roux can be likened to the shade of your skin, mine being caramel- colored." It has many variations in thickness and color.

* For additional flavor, add Tabasco spicy salt.

TWO

SURPRISE – BIRTHING A CHAMPION

I attended nursery school at the Jewish Community Center (JCC) in New Orleans. Though my parents are Catholic, this wonderful school, with its community center, pool, gym, and basketball court, was part of our history. When my siblings and I were young, my father played basketball there and my mom played racquetball; we swam all summer and joined Little League programs. It had always felt like home, so when after years away I returned to New Orleans with Eli, we re-joined. At that point, we had been together for three years.

I met Eli, a former Globetrotter and semi-pro basketball player, when I was a freshman at Fashion Institute of Technology (FIT) in New York City. Fashion was my career path, but sports, which I had always loved, was still a passion. I played volleyball for FIT, and we competed all over the state. I also played in various soccer leagues in Central Park and occasionally played tennis when invited by a friend to a club, though that was more of a sport that I played with my dad or grandmother growing up. I really enjoyed playing basketball, particularly in New York City, because it was easy to find a court and a pick-up game just about anywhere. I was also a member of the Westside YMCA on 63rd Street between Central Park West and Columbus, which gave me a place to play when the weather didn't cooperate. I loved the accessibility of the sport; the only issue was that it was predominantly men playing, but I quickly learned to adapt.

The protocol for pickup games is that the next five people to sign up or show up had to play together. You didn't have a choice. Recognizing the fact that they likely didn't want a girl on their team, I'd have to find ways to excel. I knew I could wear out my opponent by outrunning them; they usually didn't want to run if they didn't have to. I was a great passer, making others look good. I learned to be a pretty good shooter as I would often be left open. I could handle the ball well enough to take it up the court if our point guard was trapped. I also happened to be a quick defender, often stealing the ball and upsetting the opponent. For all these reasons, I would develop a few regular friends at courts around the city who allowed me to play on their team. They learned how to use me as a "secret weapon" since the other team would underestimate my skills.

I had seen Eli play in Central Park, which was near where I lived, and befriended him pretty quickly. He was a playground favorite, partly because he had a big personality; plus, it helped that he had played overseas. Tall, lean, and agile, he was quick enough to handle the ball but could also shoot and rebound. He was an asset to any team. He was also very kind, friendly, and goofy. We exchanged pager numbers and would often let each other know which court and what part of town we'd be playing in. It was fun.

When he wanted to play at more renowned courts like the Cage on West 4th Street or some of the advanced courts further uptown, I traveled along just to watch him play. I was acutely aware of the limits of my skills and the players even allowed on such courts. This was fine; I just really enjoyed the sport.

Eli and I became great friends but lived very separate lives. I was still going to school and enjoying city life with my wonderful friends and roommates. I also worked as a nanny to a nine-year-old boy on the Upper East Side and spent my spare time mentoring another boy, the same age, from the Douglass Projects on 103rd and Amsterdam. Eli lived in Washington Heights and had a very different work and social life. I would later find out that he had a young daughter.

We remained long-distance friends when I graduated. Eli went back to playing basketball overseas. I had moved to Hong Kong to work and later to Los Angeles to start my own clothing line called Pooch, after the affectionate nickname I had given my little sister. A few years after I moved to California, Eli contacted me; he had returned to the States and was playing with a new league in Irvine, right near LA. That league didn't pan out, but our relationship began. I couldn't wait to take him to the Hollywood YMCA right off Sunset Blvd., where I was now a member and played regular pick-up basketball. He was immediately accepted as one of the better players and, just like that, the duo was back. We had a symbiotic style together; we would run the court, typically winning, until we got tired. He had moved into coaching and was running an after-school program in the neighborhood.

After about two years together, we decided it would be a good idea to move to New Orleans. Eli, who had never been, was particularly excited. It seemed to have some aesthetic similarities to his original home of Cuba. I knew there were plenty of youth programs he could work with and kids who needed mentoring. I wanted to open a store with my contemporary clothing line and try to bring more local manufacturing to New Orleans. When we got there, I helped him start a non-profit called "Take-Off," for taking kids off the streets; I also opened a store on Magazine Street with my friend, Babette, who was a jewelry designer. Our first fundraiser for the new non-profit "Take-Off" was a hugely successful event at a warehouse Downtown that had been converted into an event space. We held a fashion show with Pooch clothing and had a hip-hop group and popular rapper perform. Our friend Cooper Manning was the MC, and friends Ro, Jeff, Eric, and Jeremy who had a record and production company called Renaissance Records, helped host. I was three months pregnant – a happy surprise I had recently learned of – and thoroughly enjoying my work. Little did I know that these fashion fundraisers would be an integral part of what was to come.

We joined the JCC in New Orleans to have a place to continue our game. We signed up for the all-male league – they didn't have a women's league – and they really didn't want to allow me to play. They didn't have much of a choice, though, because Eli wouldn't play without me, and they definitely wanted his talent. It had to be a "package pick" in the league drafts.

After two seasons I told them that I wanted to be a captain. Captains got to draft their team and decide who started and played. I knew most of these guys. I had either grown up with them or by now had figured out their strengths and weaknesses. I believed I could put together a championship team – and they agreed to let me be captain. One of the team members I chose was an older man everyone called Doc, because he was a doctor. He was a little bit slower, but he had a secret strength: he was good at fouling and getting away with it. This was precisely why I picked him – I was always chosen to guard him when we played against him, and I was tired of being fouled.

I also picked an old high school friend, Dana, who was large enough to play low, had a lot of stamina, and was an all-around likable guy. I knew he'd bring up the team's energy. Another pick was a guy who I'd met in the league. Matt was tall with some weight on him so he could play low but he also had a great three-point shot. Another friend and draft pick was a restaurant manager, Joe, who I had met at the newly opened Herbsaint; he was great off the bench and didn't complain about it.

We were an unassuming team but had an exceptional balance of talents and everyone knew their roles.

It was May 2002, and we had made it to the semifinals of the JCC championship. No one on the team understood why I had benched myself in the second quarter – I was the captain and typically played the entirety of the games. However, my energy was waning and I was determined to win this championship.

We managed to make it to the finals, as I had predicted with this carefully chosen team. Once again, I benched myself after the first half. I was more tired than usual, and though my teammates were still puzzled no one complained about the extra playing time. As the game continued, very close in score, I watched the final minutes on the clock taper off and realized we were going to win the championship. While the playtime had drained me, it was enough to affirm that this was exactly the energy I wanted to transfer to my baby.

We went to celebrate at The Bulldog on Magazine Street, a pub we frequented after significant wins. As everyone raised their glasses to cheer, I raised my water glass and told the team about my pregnancy – even more reason to celebrate!

* * *

There have been a few times over the years when I've taken Grace-Rose to the JCC to see my name – the only female name – on the plaque on the wall. I did that to remind her that she was a champion before she was even born.

I've also made sure she knows of the strength she inherited from another champion in our family – my paternal grandmother.

Growing up, we spent summers with my grandmother in Scituate, Massachusetts. Grammy was an award-winning, record-breaking tennis, basketball, and field hockey coach. She is in the Boston University Hall of Fame, she was featured in *Sports Illustrated* when it was predominantly male, and she still holds the best record in New England for high school women's tennis. She was very disciplined, and so were our days when we visited. They consisted of breakfast, tennis, lunch, beach, more tennis, and after dinner either shooting a basketball or throwing a football in the backyard. Our only real "downtime" was when she had us sit for an hour of *Days of Our Lives* after lunch and the five p.m. *Jeopardy*, during which she would enjoy a vodka tonic. She would give us a cranberry and orange juice "treat" and each an equal amount of Cheese-Its. None of us complained about the TV shows because we didn't have a TV at home and this was an indulgence. However, we did complain about the small amount of Cheese-Its, because we were usually very hungry.

Funny side note here: when GR was in first grade one of her classmates had a crush on her. The mother found me at Back to School Night to let me know. She looked very familiar but I couldn't figure out why. When she found out I had a retail store, she mentioned her jewelry line: it was called Hope, Faith, Miracles. When I looked up the website she had sent me, I saw that it was founded by Kristian Alfonso, aka Hope Brady from *Days of our Lives*. At our next class event, I told her how *"Days"* was one of the only TV shows I knew growing up. We'd patiently wait each year until our next summer trip to find out what had transpired between Hope and Bo Brady. I also couldn't get over how she looked exactly the same!

At the age of eighty-three, my grandmother told us she had breast cancer. She was able to treat and fight it until it returned at eighty-seven, when the treatment no longer worked. As mentioned earlier, she was in hospice and near the end when Grace-Rose was born, but we faxed a photo of the newborn GR to Grammy's hospital so she was able to see her first great-grandchild.

When GR was in the NICU, fighting her way into this world, I was acutely aware that Grammy was fighting her way out. I truly believe that when she passed away on Christmas – the day after GR came home from the hospital – she passed on her champion spirit. It felt as though Grammy had waited for GR to come home before finally letting go.

In the days, weeks, and years that followed, this belief – that GR was born with an inherent fight and spirit – brought me some measure of comfort.

King Cake

A New Orleans King Cake is a traditional dessert associated with Mardi Gras celebrations, particularly in Louisiana. It's typically shaped into a ring or oval to symbolize a king's crown. The cake is brightly decorated with the signature Mardi Gras colors: purple (representing justice), green (representing faith), and gold (representing power).

The hidden surprise: a small plastic baby is typically tucked inside the cake. Tradition holds that whoever finds the baby in their slice is either "king" or "queen" for the day and is responsible for hosting the next King Cake party.

Cultural Significance:

The King Cake is tied to the Christian celebration of Epiphany (also known as King's Day or Twelfth Night), which marks the visit of the Three Wise Men to Baby Jesus. The cakes are typically enjoyed from January 6 (Epiphany) through Mardi Gras (the day before Lent begins).

Ingredients:

For the Dough:

- 3 1/2 cups (440 g) all-purpose flour
- 1/4 cup (50 g) granulated sugar
- 1 packet (2 1/4 tsp) active dry yeast
- 1/2 tsp salt
- 1/2 cup (120 ml) warm milk (110°F or 43°C)
- 1/4 cup (60 ml) warm water
- 1/4 cup (55 g) unsalted butter, melted

- 2 large eggs
- 1 tsp vanilla extract

For the Filling:

- 1/2 cup (100 g) brown sugar
- 1 tbsp ground cinnamon
- 1/4 cup (55 g) unsalted butter, softened

For the Glaze:

- 1 cup (120 g) powdered sugar
- 2-3 tbsp milk
- 1/2 tsp vanilla extract

For Decoration:

- Purple, green, and gold (yellow) sanding sugar
- Optional: A small plastic baby (to hide inside the cake)

Instructions:

1. Activate the yeast:

   In a small bowl, combine warm water, warm milk, and yeast. Let sit for 5 minutes until foamy.

2. Make the dough:

   In a large mixing bowl, combine flour, sugar, and salt. Add the yeast mixture, melted butter, eggs, and vanilla. Mix until the dough forms a sticky ball. Knead on a floured surface for 8-10 minutes until smooth and elastic. (Or use a stand mixer with a dough hook for 5-7 minutes.)

3. Let the dough rise:

   Place the dough in a greased bowl, cover, and let it rise in a warm spot for about 1 hour, or until it doubles in size.

4. Prepare the filling:

    In a small bowl, mix brown sugar, cinnamon, and soft-
    ened butter into a paste.

5. Assemble the King Cake:
    *   Roll out the dough into a large rectangle (about 10x16
        inches).
    *   Spread the filling evenly over the dough.
    *   Roll it tightly into a log from the long side, then shape
        it into a ring. Pinch the ends together to seal.
    *   Place the ring on a greased baking sheet. Cover and
        let rise for another 30 minutes.

1. Bake the cake:

    Preheat the oven to 375°F (190°C). Bake for 20-25 min-
    utes, or until golden brown. Cool completely.

2. Hide the baby (optional):

    If using a plastic baby carefully tuck it into the underside
    of the cooled cake.

3. Make the glaze:

    Mix powdered sugar, milk, and vanilla until smooth. Driz-
    zle over the cake.

4. Decorate:

    Sprinkle the purple, green, and gold sugars over the glaze
    in alternating sections

* It's not common to add salt to king cakes but sprinkling a
little Flaky sea salt on top can enhance the sweetness

THREE

GR4CF – FUNDRAISING

If God loves everyone, why would He give me CF?

Gradually, I started getting used to our new normal: the constant daily monitoring of how Grace-Rose was feeling, digesting, and breathing, coupled with daily doses of medications, nebulizer treatments, and doctors' appointments.

Ever present in my mind was figuring out how I was going to do this on my own – all, of course, while continuing to work.

The most challenging part of this new normal was knowing that GR could face a life-threatening crisis at any moment. At five months old, she was readmitted to the hospital with a liver scare – there was even talk of her needing a transplant. I recall sitting next to her and holding her tiny hand while they scanned her body. Had I administered the ursodiol wrong? Was it my fault? Fortunately, the scans came back clear and I was told to continue the liver medications with an additional daily dose.

At nine months old, she would be tested to see if the enzymes were working properly. Again, she'd be forced into a tiny little tube where we'd have to wait for a laser light to pass through her intestines.

What became more overwhelming was figuring out the insurance plan, as my first two medical bills came in around $200,000.

I was self-employed and self-insured, but that wasn't going to pay those bills. This didn't even start to cover the monthly medications, home health care, routine Cystic Fibrosis clinics, or future doctor visits. I also had a career that was driven solely by me and my ability to bring in more sales. This would become less of a priority. I could no longer run a store, but fortunately websites and the internet were becoming more of a thing. I decided to create a website and start a baby and children's clothing line to accompany my contemporary clothing line for women. I now had an in-house model. Since my current line was already being sold in boutiques, the website would allow me to do more wholesale.

Amidst all of this, I had a growing desire to do something proactive about CF. It seemed that much of the fundraising for research and development for new medications and a cure was being done by individuals with or connected to CF – likely because it was a relatively rare, unknown disease. Raising awareness, therefore, was critical to helping the Foundation and organizations providing the resources.

Only 30,000 Americans and 70,000 people worldwide at the time had CF. As a result, it's considered an "orphan disease," meaning it is under-researched because it's not as profitable to treat. When GR was born, people with CF were not living very long; also, their quality of life was often poor, with rapidly declining lung function. The disease was described as if you were "slowly suffocating" or "trying to breathe through a straw." For all of these reasons, we needed to become part of the fight.

I had always believed that putting positive energy toward something could only result in a positive outcome. I had also always been a fan of "giving back" in some form. In college, I'd mentored Jamie, a young boy living in the projects and in desperate need of someone to help keep him on the right track. My time and energy spent with Jamie gave him other outlets and resources and led to future mentors for him to help ensure that he wouldn't become another statistic.

I raised funds for inner-city youth programs and even co-founded a non-profit to support one. I had always used my creativity and ties to the fashion world to spark fresh, engaging ways for people to get involved. This would prove to be no different with CF.

The more I had read about CF and its community and fundraising strategies, the more I became inspired to do something myself.

The hospital had given me a VHS (videotape) upon discharge, to watch and further educate myself about the disease. It featured Boomer Esiason and his son, Gunnar. Gunnar was about eight years older than GR, but they were our introduction to CF life and raising money and awareness. Fortunately, Boomer was a celebrity, a former NFL quarterback, who was willing to use his voice and connections to help. It was inspiring. I would use whatever connections and voice I had to help as well.

I started planning a fashion show fundraiser, figuring this would be more fun to attend than the usual sit-down dinners. I wanted to quite literally "breathe more life" into the event. I could use the creative approach to sell more tickets, raise money, and bring more awareness to this "orphan disease." Producing such an ambitious event would mean more work on my end, but I believed that was necessary to gain the interest and support we needed. It also gave me a way to channel my frustrations into something more productive.

It was something I could do that helped me feel in charge of a situation that was entirely the opposite.

I connected with the local foundation, then got down to work. The first step was enlisting the help of friends as volunteers in every capacity. My friend's record and promoting company would help us secure liquor sponsors, an MC, and a DJ. Our friends at Rubensteins, a local family-run department store, would be the clothing sponsor. My father had developed a brand-new condominium building on St. Charles Avenue in downtown New Orleans. It has several amenities, including a large event space on the lobby floor, that was donated for us to use. Popular chefs Susan Spicer, Donald Link, and John Harris all agreed to donate food. We gathered amazing silent auction items from friends, artists, and businesses around the city and asked local celebrities to participate. Several Hornets (now the Pelicans) players, including Birdman and our rookie, JR Smith, would model clothes, as well as Helena Moreno and the Mackel twins from Channel 6 News. The cover of *The Times Pica-yune* featured an article titled "Local Designer Rallies Celebrity Models for a Benefit Fashion Show" with a photo of me and GR.

The theme of the event was Cole Porter. Harry Connick Sr., our local DA and father of Harry Connick Jr., had his own band and per-formed Cole Porter songs throughout the night. We have a sweet photo memory of Harry Connick Sr. holding GR and serenading her. At the end of the event, GR took it upon herself to strut down the runway, solo, something she had clearly been practicing during the event pro-duction setup. Upon reaching the end of the runway, little eighteen month old GR shouted "Thank YOU," garnering smiles and laughter from everyone in the room.

After cleaning and totaling the funds raised, I crossed the street to Mike's on the Avenue, where guests, models, foundation executives, and sponsors had gathered for an after-party. When I walked in, the entire place erupted in a standing ovation. I was totally caught off guard, incredibly flattered, and completely hooked.

Since I was in the fashion business and these events were fashion-focused, I would encourage GR to be involved in whatever capacity she wanted. From her earliest days she had accompanied me to fabric stores, and she always wanted to touch and feel the different materials. She was also, from a young age, incredibly picky about what she wore. Even before she could speak, she would tug at her neck if I put a turtleneck on her. She always threw hats off her head and she despised smocking, which was common in the South. She would rub her chest incessantly until I removed it. As a result, I would always allow her to design her own outfits for these special events.

In the meantime, I was dealing with the daily reality of managing GR's condition. Again, websites were just becoming popular, which was an incredible blessing, allowing me to sell Pooch Clothing wholesale and retail from anywhere. I could keep a constant eye on GR and administer whatever meds she needed at any time of the day. Plus, if she wasn't well or had been up all night, I could be more attentive to those needs.

GR grew up in the fashion world. She traveled with me to showrooms in New York, trade shows in Las Vegas, and was a fixture on my hip in sales meetings.

She loved the softness in the tees I created and would later use these blanks to start her very first t-shirt line, Somage, named after her goldfish.

Somage was her first pet and a gift I had given her when her first sickness came on. Doctors kept saying she would get constant colds and possible infections. I didn't know how much to isolate her from germs or expose her to build her resistance. Either way, when her first serious cold developed at eighteen months old, I thought to myself, *This is the beginning.*

I felt so bad seeing her this uncomfortable, I wanted to do or give her something to cheer her up. A puppy was out of the question and the family cat was certainly no consolation, given her advanced age and feisty demeanor. GR thought all cats scratched when you went to pet them. I made an effort to keep the two apart. A fish seemed like a decent compromise, so I brought home a beautiful purple and blue iridescent one. In truth, it was less about the color and more that the Petco rep said a beta fish would "last much longer than a traditional goldfish."

When I asked her what she would like to name it, GR replied, "Somage" without hesitation, as though she had been waiting for just the right opportunity. (GR had an affinity for creating "S" names. Her first doll, a special gift from my aunt, she named Sandesta.)

When my dad heard about the fish's unusual name, he predicted that she wouldn't remember it in the morning. The following day she went to check on her fish and said, "Good mornin', Somage." He was shocked.

GR's first t-shirt line would be a blank tee of her choice. And whenever I went fabric shopping, I'd allow her to choose a fish applique – be it satin, sequin, rhinestone, etc. We would then sew it onto the tee shirt and have an embroiderer stitch "Somage" underneath. It only made sense to have her help design her outfits for the fundraisers. This would give her something fun and creative to do and foster a positive association with the concept of fundraising and awareness.

For the Cole Porter event, we had already come up with the concept for the T-shirt, a white tee with GR4CF (Grace Rose 4 Cystic Fibrosis) written in rhinestones to accompany her custom "blinged out" white converse. GR4CF would become the moniker for all events moving forward. She chose a white linen material for the skirt with netting to go underneath to make it "poofy" and a satin silver ribbon trim around the bottom.

It was not long after the first event that we began planning our next one, thanks to a recently formed alliance with the New Orleans CF Chapter. The black and white Capote-style ball would be held at the newly opened Ritz Carlton and include some Saints football players, as well as Rubensteins fashion and local entertainment.

For this event GR, then two-and-a-half, picked out some beautiful, large, beaded roses to be placed on the top part of her gown; the bottom would consist of layers of asymmetrical black and red tulle to match the colorful beaded roses. I could tell she felt like a princess because while the MC, one of our Saints players, was welcoming guests, she began to strut up and down the runway twirling in her gown, unknowingly upstaging him.

We got a spot on the local news to promote the event. This was GR's first televised appearance, and I recall wondering why Eric Paulson was having a hard time getting through the interview without laughing. Later, I saw that GR, who was sitting on my lap, had been making silly faces directly into the camera, trying to draw attention and lighten the mood. She was clearly comfortable on set, unlike myself – I've never quite gotten accustomed to it. At one point he looked directly at GR and said, "I can tell you're gonna be a star."

It would not be the last time I heard this.

In the many themed fashion fundraisers that followed, GR and I settled into a comfortable rhythm. I used my creativity and connections;

GR used her voice and stage presence to help bring awareness and raise money for this disease.

Each summer, we would plan another event, choosing friends' venues that would be generously donated, including Republic, Cap du Ville, Martine Chaisson Gallery, Loft 523, International House Hotel, Rice Mill Lofts rooftop, and others, with our wonderful local chefs helping out.

Cannata's, our friend's grocery and bakery, always contributed amazing baked goods. We'd engage local musicians, celebrities, and anyone else who wanted to participate and volunteer. For several years Rubensteins would supply the clothing for the runway, and my friend, Lisa, who worked at Saks, would donate gift bags with an assortment of samples. We'd ask friends who were artists or owned stores and restaurants to participate in the silent auction. It was a city-wide, group effort, indeed.

Each year, this was something fun for me to plan with GR. We'd start by discussing the themes; one year was ice-cream-themed and the models wore upside-down cone hats on their heads with melting ice cream makeup; another theme was "Broadway," and GR performed, along with our singer-friend, Anais. One theme was "Pink," and everyone was encouraged to wear the color. All the drinks and treats were pink, and GR specifically requested a large cotton candy machine as the focal point of the event.

Event planning gave us something to look forward to and discuss at length, serving as a healthy distraction. We'd talk about how to lay out the venue and fashion show, what the makeup would look like, the decor, the invites, the music, food, and the models. Each and every part was carefully considered, as this was very important to GR. When she wasn't feeling well or had extra time-consuming treatments to do, this gave us a creative, positive, and sedentary thing to focus on. And, when her health was worsening, this was our way of fighting back.

GR was four years old when I was invited, by the CEO of the New Orleans CF chapter, to my first Volunteer Leadership Conference (VLC) conference. We had recently moved to Los Angeles, but I believe the New

Orleans CF chapter thought we'd be returning soon – as did I – especially since GR and I had continued our events in New Orleans each summer.

The VLC is a huge conference held in Washington, DC. All the major volunteers across the country attend so they can learn better fundraising techniques; it also motivates them to continue. Successful volunteers – all of whom are parents or close relatives of people with CF – share their input. Medical professionals from the Bethesda Cystic Fibrosis Foundation headquarters attend to share what to expect in the 'pipeline' and on the horizon regarding drugs and research.

When I arrived, I was surprised to see how many couples were attending together. *Must be nice,* I thought, *to have someone else that understands exactly what you're up against. A partner in this.*

I also heard stories of one parent having to quit their job to become the full-time caregiver or how the family had to move to be closer to a CF care center or downsize in order to afford the medical bills. This all started hitting me in a way I hadn't really had time to think about before. Life kept throwing me curveballs; I was just trying to keep up. The overwhelming individual responsibility of this started to sink in.

I recall a mother, Margarete Cassalina, who I am still connected with on social media, getting up to speak. She had two children with CF and had just lost her twelve-year-old daughter, Jena. She was fundraising and fighting on behalf of a life left behind and a life still ahead. Having two children with CF was unfathomable, but her courage to get up and speak about such an enormous loss left an indelible mark on me. I knew her strength was coming from her need to encourage her son and everyone else in the room to keep fighting.

Former sports newscaster and writer Frank De Ford spoke on behalf of his daughter, Alex, who he had lost in 1980 when she was eight years old. Afterward, he gave me a copy of his book, *Alex: The Life of a Child.* I had a hard time reading it. I'm sure it was brilliant, but like every other book recommendation and inspiring reference I was receiving, it was about loss and grief. I didn't want these emotions taking up more space than the will to live and fight. After the event, I retreated to my hotel room, depleted and terrified, yet completely motivated.

* * *

GR, my sister Kate, and I were all in the bathroom getting ready for GR4CF #8. We were listening to music, doing our hair and makeup, and getting excited for this year's event. We were already anticipating the outcome of all our hard work.

Eight-year-old Grace-Rose suddenly turned to me and asked, as if she had been contemplating it for some time, "Mom, if God loves everybody, why would He give me CF?"

Caught off guard and feeling a subtle gaze coming from my sister, I needed an answer, quickly. Before I knew it, the words were flowing, as if I'd been asked this before.

"I know it may be hard to understand right now, but it's because you are special, you were chosen. You have a strong personality and a loud voice. He chose you to be able to do the exact work you're doing right now, to speak up on behalf of those who can't. It's like my friend Daniel, whose family you know."

Daniel was an incredible person and a talented artist who had been senselessly murdered at a young age. His parents started fundraising on behalf of NOCCA, the art school he attended, for scholarships to give to young aspiring artists like him. They had taken something tragic and turned it into something beautiful.

"I truly believe," I told GR, "that you're going to help the CF Community find a cure."

Thankfully, that seemed to satisfy her for the time being. A year later, right after GR4CF #9, GR said, "Mom, I want to design the next collection for the runway and have kids my age modeling."

I looked at my daughter, soon to be ten years old, and was awestruck by her drive and passion. How could I possibly say no?

Chicken Tender and Caesar Salad Po'Boy

A twist on New Orleans po'boys (typically fried shrimp, fried oyster, or roast beef)

This one includes chicken tenders, a high-calorie food GR loved as a child, combined with her favorite Caesar salad from the London Hotel in West Hollywood.

French Bread

Warm Chicken Tenders

Caesar Salad – use the smaller leaves of the romaine lettuce (uncut), add your favorite Caesar dressing (or make your own) and add parmesan.

Slice and warm the french bread, add a little butter on each side of the bread, and assemble the warm chicken tenders, with the Caesar salad romaine leaves in between.

* Add a little garlic or celery salt to the salad to increase flavor

FOUR

KATRINA – STORM

In August of 2005, shortly after our black and white Capote-themed event at the Ritz, we were told a storm was coming. This is fairly common at the height of hurricane season in New Orleans. However, as the storm got larger and closer and seemed like it would be a direct hit, people were advised to begin evacuating immediately.

During hurricane season, people stock up so they're always prepared for a storm. They buy excess water and canned goods, candles, and flashlights. Some have backup generators, some board up windows, etc.

These storms occur frequently and typically knock out electricity, with heavy winds doing some damage to trees. Those who feel they're in a relatively safe area usually stay in town to "ride it out," so long as they have the necessary provisions. This is New Orleans, after all; people welcome any reason to stay home from work and drink, play games, and socialize. They're affectionately known as "hurricane parties."

On the other hand, a lot of people leave town and sit in hours of traffic just to reach the next closest city that may be out of the storm's reach. Typically, people head toward Houston, only to end up turning right back around once the storm passes with minimal damage.

My family and I always stayed put, but this storm was different. The mayor was strongly encouraging people to leave town. Now, with one day before the eye of the storm was due to hit, he ordered a mandatory evacuation. At this point the people who hadn't already evacuated had to make an instant decision: sit in the crawling, practically gridlocked traffic, or stay and risk their lives. Most people left; those who could not afford or otherwise lacked the ability to leave were informed to go to the Superdome, our NFL arena; they were told it was a safe haven. My parents, GR, and I decided to stay in their condo in the new building downtown that my dad had developed. We were joined by my younger sister, Kate, who had just returned from her college graduation in California, and my brother, Mac, who had returned to New Orleans after living in Germany.

Waiting the storm out in the building made the most sense. The windows were storm-proof, there was a backup generator, the twenty-four-hour security team was staying, and the entire building was locked up. Plus, I had GR's medical equipment and meds to manage and I didn't want to get stuck on the road with her. Should there be a power outage, GR would be able to use her nebulizer to do her breathing treatments with the backup generator.

We were joined by my uncle, his wife, and their daughter, as well as two of my friends who hadn't had enough time to leave. All the other residents of the building had left, except the Olivers' across the hall. Bill Oliver was the president of AT&T and needed to be on ground zero for communications reasons.

We tied up the glass doors to the terrace just in case and watched as the wicked storm and winds began to blow across the sky. GR, just two and a half years old, had no idea if this was nervous, terrifying, or exciting energy. Whatever it was, she certainly felt it, and scurried around in anticipation. We waited in the staircase as the storm passed to ensure no broken glass or building damage would strike us. When the worst of it was over, we returned to the living room and could see curtains swinging out of windows from the Intercontinental Hotel a few blocks away, as well as debris below from the items that had been thrown out. A little bit further away, we noticed part of the roof had been torn off the Superdome, where so many people had fled as a makeshift shelter.

It wasn't until hours later that we ventured outside to witness the damage. This was not a safe decision, but we were anxious to get some (not so) fresh air. We saw old buildings that had crumbled, several trees that had been knocked down, and powerlines strewn across the ground. We walked by Saks Fifth Avenue and Brooks Bros., with their front windows shattered but mannequins and displays still intact. It wasn't until we started seeing cars racing toward Walmart and drugstores that we realized things were being looted. It was only a matter of time before it started happening at some of these other locations. We recognized the disparity, desperation, and dangerous nature of the situation. Quickly returning to the condo, we found my mother cooking bacon – more out of a need to expend her nervous energy than hunger. Thankfully, we had a gas stove and what seemed to be an enormous supply of bacon. We would later reminisce amusingly over the copious amounts we ingested during that time.

With no access to media coverage, the only news we were hearing was from our neighbor, who was in communication with the mayor. So we were surprised later that afternoon to see water seeping up Poydras Street. The storm had passed and dried up, so where could it be coming from? This is when we learned that the levees broke.

We had been sleeping outside on the terrace, which despite the heat still felt cooler than being inside with no AC. I noticed GR's cough becoming much more consistent. Her body was acutely sensitive to heat and dehydration, but also the unhealthy particles floating in the air. Her nebulizer no longer worked as the backup generator had expired. We hadn't planned for this long.

When we looked over the balcony, we could see droves of people making their way from the Superdome to the Convention Center, seeking food, water, assistance, and a solid roof over their heads. We also saw people coming out of the flooded streets, soaking wet, looking for aid. We would later find out that portions of the city were not just severely flooded, but underwater.

People were trapped in their homes – in attics or on rooftops. Those not fortunate enough to be rescued were floating lifeless in the flooded streets. The situation was frightening, horrific, and growing worse by the minute.

GR was now overheating and struggling to breathe. I told my parents I needed to get her to an air-conditioned place with electricity. Initially, they objected, concerned for our safety. Not only did we not know which bridges or outlets were accessible, but people were so desperate to get out that they were jumping on any car they saw leaving. Then, shortly after my decision to go, the mayor told our neighbor that we all needed to leave. It was too unsafe.

I packed an overnight bag; all of GR's meds and necessary equipment; her favorite doll, Sandesta; her beta fish, Somage (who ended up in a ziplock bag), and the family cat, Ann, who was very old. I also grabbed any small necessary provisions, like her favorite books to read on the road. Kate and Mom joined us, while my father and brother took a separate car. My uncle and his family took their own car, and before they left he handed me a shotgun. He was the hunting and fishing type of uncle. When I expressed reluctance – I'd never held a gun before – he insisted; we were a car full of women and a baby who could possibly be attacked while driving out. I took it, my hand shaking, and tucked it under my seat. I had no idea how to use it.

Our caravan of four cars, led by our neighbor, drove to the only overpass that was not damaged or underwater. My car was in the middle for extra protection. As we got on the desolate highway headed toward Lafayette, there were droves of National Guard vehicles headed into town directly where we had exited, next to the Superdome and Convention Center. We assumed they were going to aid the stranded victims. It wasn't until we got to Lafayette and found an open lunch spot to order some food that we saw the news for the first time. I remember all of us just staring, mouths agape and tears streaming down our faces, at the TV. The devastation was like nothing we had ever seen and left us speechless, even as we headed back on the road to find a place to sleep.

We found a hotel in Houston that by some miracle had a vacant room. The first thing we did when we checked in, even before we started GR's treatment, was to unleash Somage into the coffee pot that we filled with water so she could swim. We spent the night flipping from one news channel to another and not understanding why the reports were saying no food or water had been delivered to the desperate people who remained. What about all those government vehicles we had seen streaming into town hours earlier? We later heard about frustrated citizens who returned to take out their pirogues or canoes and start rescuing people on their own.

Houston was so overcrowded that we decided to continue to San Antonio, the next closest city. On the way we stopped at a Target to buy some clothes since none of us had packed for much more than an overnight. As we were walking through the store, the song *Since You've Been Gone by* Kelly Clarkson came on. This was one of GR's favorite songs. A consummate entertainer, she grabbed a nearby chrome toilet paper stand, lifted it onto a small platform and started belting out the song. I wasn't sure whether to applaud or hide. After San Antonio, we stopped in a small town that happened to be full of crickets. GR referred to it as "cricket Texas," crickets were everywhere, including the hotel room. GR and the cat, Ann, thought it was "fun" and spent the majority of the time trying to catch them. My mom, sister, and I couldn't find a high enough place to sit, eat, or sleep because they jumped all over everyone and everything. None of the locals seemed to mind, but we certainly weren't going to stay there. We decided to head to Phoenix – or "pancake Phoenix" – as GR referred to it, since she recalls being promised the treat when we got there. On the way, I was pulled over for speeding. When the police officer saw my plates, she said "Oh, you're just trying to get the hell out of there!" and let me go without a ticket.

We took turns sitting in the back seat with GR, reading *Silly Sally*, her favorite book of the trip. I lost count how many hours this went on; all I will say is that we can recite this book by heart. In fact, GR would one day use it as a prompt for one of her college admissions essays.

As we headed West, I said to Mom, "Let's go visit Alli," my older sister, who lived in Los Angeles and had an infant. "No way are we going that far," Mom replied, "We're going home." That, unfortunately, was not an option. We did end up going to Los Angeles, and here we are twenty years later.

To this day, I still don't understand why help wasn't received sooner. The aftermath of Katrina permeated every household, community, and business.

People weren't allowed to return to the city unless they had a business to check on or were helping with basic needs and supplies. Others couldn't return because their homes had been destroyed.

The devastation would have a lasting effect that forever changed the landscape of the city. Even now, two decades later, people always refer to New Orleans in context, as "Before the Storm" and "After the Storm."

Although the heart of the city could not be destroyed, we certainly lost some of its soul.

Bacon-Wrapped Scallops

GR loved this dish but now prefers it wrapped in prosciutto or turkey bacon since she stopped eating bacon. (During the storm, my mom cooked copious amounts of bacon.)

Use large scallops, pre-cook the bacon until it's cooked but still soft.

I like to dry off the scallops by adding salt and patting them with a paper towel to absorb the excess water.

Spray one side of the scallops with cooking olive oil spray and place that side down in a super- hot skillet.

Spray the top of the exposed scallops and turn them (about 1 minute each side) to get them brown. Wrap bacon around each scallop and place a toothpick to secure it.

Place the bacon-wrapped scallops into a baking pan and stick it in the oven for about 20 minutes or until bacon is crispy.

I like to serve them on a bed of something colorful like sweet pea mashed potatoes.

Take mashed potatoes and add a can of sweet peas, draining the water but leaving a little bit to soften the consistency. Blend them in a food processor or something similar and add butter and salt.

You can also use sweet potato, squash, or purple cauliflower puree, depending on the color you want.

Add a dollop of sriracha mixed with horseradish mayo on top of each scallop for a little "kick" or plain sriracha. Top with microgreens such as broccoli, arugula, or daikon.

* For even more color and additional flavor, sprinkle Kala Na-mak (aka black salt) on top.

FIVE

LOS ANGELES – BIG MOVE

Five days after the storm, we arrived at my sister's house in the Hollywood Hills. By then, Grace-Rose's cough had become so consistent that even her treatments and medications weren't helping and I knew I had to get her to a medical facility right away. An ER at Kaiser on Sunset immediately prescribed steroids, which seemed to settle the cough a little.

We had met Alli's baby, Zander, five months earlier during a planned visit. This time, we descended on them with no idea how long we would stay. It was a lot, with Mom just staring at the TV in tears, GR's medical routine, and our old and rather moody cat that we had to keep separated from the two cats they had. Within a week we were handed a brochure for an Oakwood housing complex in Burbank. It was the closest facility that had fully furnished living accommodations and was commonly used by the Disney, Warner Bros., and Paramount studios (all nearby) as a place for the actors to live while auditioning or filming for pilot season.

We also noticed a lot of young kids who had come from different parts of the country to audition for networks like Nickelodeon and Disney. In fact, one day we ventured into the onsite cafeteria only to see a wall full of young kids' headshots.

When I brought GR to the pool a kid swam up to her and asked who she was and what she was there for. In other words, "Are you an actor and what are you auditioning for?" It felt a little unsettling. She simply responded with "I'm Grace-Rose" and swam away. While she may not have understood his intent, I quickly realized this was not the environment we were seeking. Also, since we had not been placed in the fully furnished apartment by a network, it was very expensive.

We were now in the month of September and school had already begun. This added another layer of heartbreak to Katrina. Up to that point, GR had attended a small Spanish school in New Orleans three half-days a week. She loved it, and I'd hoped it would help her Spanish since her father only communicated with her this way. However, before the storm, I had registered her to start nursery school in September at the JCC, where I had gone to nursery and pre-k and where one of our favorite teachers remained. I was so excited for GR to have this same experience in a wonderful, loving community of friends.

Since schools hadn't reopened, I needed to find her a local school, at least temporarily, while also doing research for a new medical team. We weren't returning to New Orleans anytime soon, and neither were GR's doctors. We had already had several scares and hospital visits for a potential liver transplant due to her jaundice as a baby, possible sinus surgeries for nasal polyps and obstruction, and issues with her pancreatic insufficiency.

These surgeries had been avoided and we were treating all of the conditions. However, I was aware that in order to receive insurance and all the prescribed daily medications and inhaled treatments, we would need a CF care center for the required quarterly hospital visits. And, of course, we'd need a team for any unforeseen circumstances. What I was starting to learn with this disease was that an infection, blockage, or other terrifying "event" could come at any time – and easily land her in the hospital for days or weeks.

I found a JCC on the West Side. I was thinking we might want to be closer to the ocean as I had recently learned that ocean air is great for CF lungs. In fact, one of her prescribed inhalants was a saline solution. We would end up making beach outings a weekend tradition – Paradise Cove, a hidden beach in Malibu for picnics and swinging on the rings next to the Santa Monica pier were among her favorites. She even tried surfing, but the moment a baby sea otter popped up on her board she bolted out of the water, assuming it was a shark. She never fully recovered.

When we visited the Westside JCC, the director immediately welcomed us, took us on a tour, and brought us into her office to discuss the schedule. GR could start right away. The school went so far as to offer us a full scholarship so the cost wouldn't be an additional burden, given our uncertain future. As we started to fill out the paperwork, the director asked if there was any additional pertinent information to share.

I replied, "Oh, yes, Grace-Rose has Cystic Fibrosis, but I am managing it with daily treatments and medications. In fact, I can show up at snack or lunchtime to administer her meds."

As soon as I said this, I could see the director's expression change. She said, "I'm so sorry, but unfortunately we have another student here with Cystic Fibrosis and, with strict instructions by the parents, no one else with CF is allowed to attend the pre-school."

I didn't quite understand why; I was learning so much about this disease on a daily basis. The director asked me if we had a CF care center yet and, if not, would I like to be put in contact with these parents? She actually called the mother right then and there so I could speak with her.

The mom explained that her child had a breathing apparatus and a lung infection that could be contagious. She also made me aware of the fact that CF patients could not be around one another due to the fact that these lung infections, of which there are four main strains, are invisible but can be lethal to the patient. They had no way of treating certain strains and some of these infections would hasten the decline of their ability to breathe. The mother then recommended her CF care team at Cedars Sinai and wished me the best. As I was processing this information, the director, sensing my concerns, mentioned that there was another JCC in the Valley and she would be happy to send us there. In gratitude, we drove over Laurel Canyon and into a neighborhood called Sherman Oaks. I had lived in L.A. before but hadn't spent time there. Though it was a bit farther than where we were staying, the wonderful school and welcoming community was worth it.

We started immediately. Grace-Rose was happy to have some structure, and I would show up daily to make sure she was taking her enzymes with food. If enzymes were ever forgotten with anything other than water, her stomach would bloat and she would be in a lot of abdominal pain. We would have to administer laxatives and wait for the pain to subside. This could sometimes take a full day, causing us to lose valuable caloric intake. I had been told the importance of a diet high in calories and fat due to the lack of absorption. I had enzymes everywhere – in the glove compartment, in all of my purses, at school, at my sister's house, even in small pouches in my pockets. If I saw her grab a banana or even a glass of milk, I would stop her to make sure she had the right number of pills before ingesting it.

This JCC was a mostly Hebrew-speaking community, and GR and I participated in the Friday shabbats where she proudly sang Hebrew songs. We would always purchase a loaf of freshly baked challah bread, or, as GR called it, "challah back bread" after the popular Gwen Stefani song, "Hollaback, Girl."

She loved Gwen Stefani, as well as Pink, and Outkast; they always got her dancing in her car seat, mostly shaking her butt back and forth. Gwen more or less taught her how to spell bananas when she was two years old. She would sing along, "B-N-A-N-A-N-S," and we thought it was too cute to correct her.

We celebrated Passover and Purim. In fact, for those two years of preschool, GR would call me "Ima," the Hebrew word for mother.

I was thrilled that GR was enjoying school and developing friendships. I especially loved how she was greeted with hugs by all the other kids each morning, as if they hadn't just seen each other the day before. I would often ask the teachers how her day was, and if it wasn't so great they would tell me, "Sometimes she wakes up from her nap a little sad and talks about missing her cat."

Anne had escaped one day while we were at Oakwood housing. By the time we realized it and had searched the enormous grounds and placed signs everywhere, we knew it was a lost cause. She was very old and likely rattled by this drastic change, so we figured she went off to rest. She was not very nice to GR and would often scratch her, but for some reason she took that as a loving gesture. She was very sad that Anne was no longer around, and when she talked about it I assumed that was her way of also describing her larger feelings of loss.

Often, when children are very young and can't fully understand or describe their feelings, they use objects and pets to help express them. We had all experienced significant upheaval recently, and GR was likely expressing her sadness about that, as well as about Anne.

As for me, it would take many years to come to terms with this new normal.

A few months after we moved into Oakwood (and realizing that we would at least stay through the school year), it was time to start looking for a more habitable place for us all to coexist.

During my initial meetings with GR's new medical team, they asked me what else I was doing other than giving her enzymes, medications, and nebulizer treatments. They asked why I didn't have the vest. Vest therapy consists of wearing a high-frequency chest wall oscillation vest. The vest itself is worn over the chest and connected via tubing to a large medical device that uses specific hertz and frequencies to help break up and loosen mucus in the airways.

Previously, I'd been told the vest wouldn't be necessary until her symptoms worsened. The new team's response was clear: everything is essential to prevent the symptoms from worsening.

This was the moment I realized the true magnitude of my job. I was not just a caregiver; I was, as my Uncle Dean, who took care of my grandmother, would remind me, GR's medical manager as well. I needed to start doing research to stay on top of anything and everything that could help with prevention. Our insurance hadn't been sorted out yet, so they sent us, as a show of sympathy for Katrina, her first vest airway clearance system. They wanted her to start using it immediately.

When it arrived, a nurse came to show us how to use the equipment. Grace-Rose was so excited because she thought I had gotten her a karaoke machine. She put it on and sang into a toy microphone. The vest shook her voice and made it sound funny. Her humor was short-lived, as she realized it was another medical device she would need to use at least two times a day – morning and night. It would limit her energetic, restless self. It would also be one more reminder of how inhibiting this disease was.

It was in those early days of the vest when GR's father came to visit. He had been in New York during Hurricane Katrina, and now three months had passed, the longest she had gone without seeing him. He had agreed to return to New Orleans to get my mother's car and drive it to L.A. for us. He loved road trips, and he wanted to come visit GR. It was right before her third birthday, and I remember her showing him her vest while she was hooked up and singing into the microphone. She thought this new "karaoke machine" was so silly. He left a few days later, and simply vanished. We haven't seen him since.

* * *

We celebrated her third birthday at Oakwood in a small adjacent park. Close friends gathered around a picnic table with food, a Cuban doll cake and a number three piñata hanging from a nearby tree. Shortly after that, during my apartment search, I saw an ad for a lovely two-bedroom in Studio City overlooking the L.A. River. I had lived in L.A. before, but never recalled a river. It was an excellent location, close to the intersection of Laurel Canyon and Ventura Blvd, with plenty of things to do within walking distance. It also happened to be in one of the best public elementary school districts in L.A. and was closer to her pre-school in Sherman Oaks.

When we looked at the apartment, I asked the landlord where the river view was. He took us out to the balcony that overlooked a dry basin. We all had a good laugh, but decided to take the apartment anyway because the landlord was so nice and was willing to work with us if for some reason we had to break the lease (my mother was still determined to get back to New Orleans sooner rather than later.) We would spend eleven years in that apartment.

Grace-Rose and I shared a bedroom, which helped me keep a close eye on her for health reasons. I was able to help with her vest therapy, change the frequency, reset the timer, hold the nebulizer up to her if she had fallen asleep, and keep her head propped up so that she could sleep more comfortably. She had so many sinus issues and trouble breathing that she would frequently cough non-stop throughout the night and I would just try to find ways to comfort her.

Getting up early for school in the mornings was always difficult. She consistently had stomach issues. Finding the right combination of medications to help her digest food was a challenge. She often started the day with severe stomach pain or blockage. This would be even more problematic because she wouldn't want to eat. A heavy, high calorie breakfast was required. If she'd been coughing throughout the night, I'd hate to wake her once she had finally found some rest. I was constantly looking for more ways to ease her discomfort. I was open to holistic options, supplements, and such, as long as it didn't interfere with what she was already taking. I could only see this getting more challenging as the disease progressed.

A huge issue with Cystic Fibrosis, due to the blocked pancreas, is the inability to gain weight. GR's BMI (body mass index) was always one of the first things we discussed in the clinic. I was always feeding her, yet she was always in the low percentile. The nutritionist on the team would then tell me more about high-fat, high-calorie diets.

I should always add more butter and more salt – always more salt because of the excessive salt loss through their sweat which would cause dehydration. This would also cause intestinal blockages and more stomach pain. The goal was to get to five thousand calories a day. They would recommend fast food such as McDonald's, shakes filled with chocolate and extra peanut butter, added caloric powders, higher-calorie ice creams, etc. They even told us about a higher-calorie peanut butter cup that was available at Costco. When GR was three-and-a-half years old, I asked the nutritionist at one of her clinics, "What about future diabetes, heart disease, and cholesterol?"

The nutritionist looked directly at both of us and said, "We don't worry about that because they don't live that long."

This was one of those moments when it hit me just how alone I was on this journey. It was already hard enough to be told I had to feed her junk food all day, every day, just to get her weight up. But what I couldn't handle was medical professionals constantly telling me my daughter wouldn't live very long - and even more so, I couldn't bear the thought of Grace-Rose having to hear this over and over.

Animal Style Sliders (Adapted from the famous IN-N-OUT Burger sauce) and Garlic Fries

An ode to the fast food she was advised to eat.

Sauce: Add ketchup, yellow mustard, pickle relish, mayonnaise, white vinegar, pepper, and (of course) salt.

Add ingredients together in a bowl to get a light orange hue. Not too much vinegar, taste for desired flavor.

You can either make your own mini patties or purchase uncooked meatballs and shape them into small patties. Cook patties, assemble on small Hawaiian buns with sauce, sliced Roma tomato, petite butter lettuce and either grilled (GR's favorite) or pickled onions.

Garlic fries -

In a bowl, combine melted butter, finely chopped garlic, parsley, and salt. Melt and place on top of (frozen) or fresh-cut fries. Cook until golden.

* Kosher salt has more adhesion to fries, can also top with parmesan

Fun fact: If you go to the IN-N-OUT Burger next to LAX (Los Angeles International Airport) you can order burgers to picnic on the adjacent lawn and watch the planes take off and land overhead.

SIX

LITTLE PRINCESS – TINY VIOLINS

"**I** want to learn the thing that goes 'ee, un, ee, un,'" GR said as she motioned with her thumb and forefinger over her left shoulder.

"Do you mean the violin?"

She nodded her head. She had been introduced to the instrument from one of her favorite cartoons, *Little Einsteins* (or, as we liked to call it, *Little Rhinestones*.) I knew the value of kids learning musical skills and how it can help with education, particularly math. It sounded like a good idea. I asked around for a local music teacher and we found one who specialized in violin and piano. I had zero experience when it came to violins. Her teacher said that since she was under the age of six, she would have to start with the Suzuki violin method and recommended a store nearby. We went to the store and asked the salesman for a violin for a three-year-old and he returned with a very small instrument, ideal for her size. When he told me the price, $525, I gasped. I had no idea how much they cost and naturally started adding up the violin, Suzuki booklets and CDs, weekly private lessons, graduating to larger violins, and so on. I wasn't even sure if she would like it.

He allowed us to rent it monthly, giving us an opportunity to return it in the event she lost interest. After almost a year of lessons, her teacher said that GR had too much energy for the violin and recommended switching to the piano for a more satisfactory experience. The violin had been paid off at this point, so we kept it. Since our apartment, and my budget, would not accommodate a piano, I instead opted for a large keyboard from the Guitar Shop. It would be her fourth birthday present.

I remember my mom asking me, "Why do you feel the need to make these big purchases for her birthdays?"

It had been a financial stretch for me at the time. My mind drifted to the obvious. It's the sense of urgency that CF instills in you. When you're constantly told about the short life expectancy, you want to seize every opportunity.

Around this time, we were in New Orleans visiting friends. One party was at our friend Terence Blanchard's house, a famous trumpet player. He chatted with GR about her interest in the violin for a while, then said, "Hold on." He returned with one of his daughter's violins that she had outgrown and told Grace-Rose she could have it. It was the next size up from hers, we were so grateful and excited.

Although her experience with the instrument was short-lived, we still have the two tiny violins.

On slow days at my retail store, GR would pull out the violin, prop the door open with her case on the ground, similar to a street performer, and begin to play. She was completely out of tune, but that didn't seem to dissuade her. With a hustle mentality as one of her innate strengths, she simply assumed she could draw an audience and bring in potential customers.

GR was a fixture in the store. Each day I would pick her up after school and bring her there until closing time. She even had a little desk in the back where she did her homework assignments. She often came out to help me merchandise the store, adding jewelry to mannequins or choosing new outfits for the window. One day a talent agent happened to be shopping in the store and took an interest in her. Never the shy one, GR struck up a conversation and the two hit it off. She asked me if my daughter had representation, and when I told her no she asked if we could set up a meeting at her office in Beverly Hills. I was a little apprehensive due to the whole CF thing. I knew GR enjoyed the camera, the stage, acting, and entertaining, but I was concerned about her health. I was also concerned about the process of auditions and rejections in general. I told the agent we would sign a contract only if she understood our situation – and that we may not always be able to make it to auditions. This wasn't ideal, but she agreed.

We went out a few times for random commercial auditions or one-liners in TV shows. Sometimes, if the drive was too far or the wait was too long, we wouldn't stay. This wasn't meant to be disrespectful, but because GR had limited time, given her treatments, meals, and homework. I also never wanted it to feel like something she had to do; we'd keep going only if it really felt exciting or fun. And when the agent started sending us out less and less, I understood.

Then a friend in the industry shared a casting for Disney Princesses. GR had recently been gifted a special birthday present: tickets to the premiere of *Princess and the Frog* at the Disney Studios in Burbank. We went to see the film, tour the studios, and visit with the animation crew, who taught her some of their drawing techniques. GR was a huge fan. I asked if she might want to audition for this new Disney Princess campaign called "Dream Big." It was an empowering message to young girls. She said yes.

In fact, another one of her favorite movies at the time was *A Little Princess* – the story of a young girl named Sara, who is sent to a strict boarding school after her father goes to serve in WWI. When he is presumed dead, the headmistress, knowing she won't receive more money from him, forces Sara to become a servant. Sara has a huge imagination and pretends she is a princess. (The theme is about the power of imagination and kindness.) Her father finally returns for her and provides the life she had dreamt. Grace-Rose would watch it over and over, I believe, imagining her father would one day return as well. She loved it so much that as a surprise one Easter, I built

her a "little princess" shrine, just as Sara had imagined. It had netting hanging from the ceiling, large Indian-inspired silk pillows, and
a treasure box with rose petals. It became her favorite place to do her
medical treatments.

* * *

When we got to the audition, GR was called into the room with several
other young girls and a casting director. Parents weren't allowed in; she
would explain to me later that she saw several other executives behind a
glass wall watching their auditions. When asked, "Which Disney princess do you relate the most to, and why?" she quickly replied, "Princess
Tiana, because she's ethnic – like me; she's from New Orleans – like me;
she's an entrepreneur – like me; and she doesn't chase after the prince
but instead has him chase after her!"

She booked it.

The date for the shoot happened to be the same weekend my
cousin Christina had insisted I join her for a girls' trip in Seattle. It
would be my first time away from GR for a full weekend. My mother
was in Los Angeles and offered to take her to the shoot so I could
enjoy the break.

It was Grace-Rose's first time working on a commercial set. Between
the wardrobe department, hair and makeup, craft services, and acting,
she was hooked. She also got excited about her first paycheck! The
director appreciated her projection and clarity so much that he asked
her to return the following day to do a voice-over. My mother thoroughly enjoyed it as well, and couldn't get over the fact that one person's
job was to hold an umbrella over GR to shade her from the sun.

In the meantime, I embarked on what was supposed to be a relaxing
spa weekend. Exactly what I needed. Little did I know that my cousin
had a different definition of "relaxing" than most. The weekend did in
fact include spa treatments, but also a professional water skier to teach
us tricks on skis. I was unaware that Christina had always wanted to
learn how to do a three-hundred-sixty-degree-spin on a single ski while

holding the rope with her toe (aka "swivel ski.") Christina's dad and my mom had grown up water skiing. In fact, my mother, one of seven, would typically be on the top of a pyramid stunt with her brothers.

Cheryl, our ski instructor, was famous for this swivel ski trick.

We had a call time of 5:30 a.m., when we were to arrive, in wet-suits, on Lake Washington. We spent two full days on the water, where, despite my best efforts, I was barely able to slalom. Christina nailed it. For our last evening she had gotten tickets to a play at the Paramount Theater in downtown Seattle and insisted we dress up as Disney princesses to attend. A very serious scientist and business-woman, she also enjoyed "make believe" and entertaining small kids in public with these antics in her downtime. When I declined the dress-up part, sarcastically noting that I did not happen to pack my Disney Princess costume, she opened a closet full of them. It was non-nego-tiable. At that moment, I couldn't help but think of the synchronicity between my weekend and GR's.

* * *

On a side note, in 2024, Terence was asked to produce the music for the new Tiana theme park at Disney World. It felt like another wonderful full- circle life moment.

Cuban Doll Cake

For GR's Birthdays we would buy or sometimes bake "Cuban Doll cakes" traditionally made with tres leches style cakes. The cake would be made as a dress around a plastic doll, to look like a princess.

Ingredients:

For the Cake:

- 2 cups (250 g) all-purpose flour
- 2 tsp baking powder
- 1/2 tsp salt
- 1/2 cup (115 g) unsalted butter, softened
- 1 cup (200 g) granulated sugar
- 5 large eggs
- 1 tsp vanilla extract

For the Tres Leches Mixture:

- 1 cup (240 ml) whole milk
- 1 cup (240 ml) sweetened condensed milk
- 1 cup (240 ml) evaporated milk

For the Whipped Cream Frosting:

- 2 cups (480 ml) heavy whipping cream
- 1/4 cup (30 g) powdered sugar
- 1 tsp vanilla extract

For Decoration:

- 1 doll cake topper (Barbie-like)
- Food coloring (optional)
- Sprinkles or edible flowers

Instructions:

1. Preheat the oven:

   Heat to 350°F (175°C). Grease and flour a dome-shaped cake pan (or use multiple round pans for stacking).

2. Make the cake batter:
   - Whisk together flour, baking powder, and salt.
   - In a separate bowl, mix cream, butter and sugar until light and fluffy. Add eggs one at a time, mixing well. Stir in vanilla extract.
   - Gradually add the dry ingredients and mix until smooth.

1. Bake the cake:

   Pour the batter into the prepared pan(s) and bake for 25-30 minutes, or until a toothpick inserted in the center comes out clean. Let the cake cool completely.

2. Soak the cake:
   - Once the cake has cooled, use a skewer or fork to poke holes all over.
   - Mix whole milk, sweetened condensed milk, and evaporated milk in a bowl. Slowly pour the mixture over the cake, allowing it to absorb fully. Chill the cake for 1-2 hours.

1. Prepare the frosting:

   Whip heavy cream, powdered sugar, and vanilla extract until stiff peaks form.

2. Assemble the doll cake:
   - Trim the soaked cake into a dome shape if needed. Insert the doll topper into the center (wrap the lower half of the doll in plastic wrap).
   - Frost the cake with whipped cream frosting. Use food coloring to tint the frosting for the "skirt" if desired.
   - Decorate with piping, sprinkles, or edible flowers.

* To intensify the sweetness, sprinkle with Vanilla flavored salt flakes

SEVEN

CARPENTER – FIRST HOSPITALIZATION

I have sweet memories of listening to little GR belting out the song "Popular" from the musical *Wicked* – which we had seen at The Pantages – on the long drives to and from the gym each day.

I was never one to remember all the words to a song. As my older sister Alli would teasingly point out, I would just make up my own. Grace-Rose, on the other hand, could recite every lyric on the *Wicked* CD – and it didn't stop there. She would continue to amaze me on those gym drives by reciting musicals in their entirety – something I would miss when I joined a gym closer to home. GR was about to start kindergarten and would require a stricter nighttime routine. We needed to save time wherever we could.

Cystic Fibrosis never takes a day off – this is a difficult truth that everyone in the CF community talks about. Each day is spent trying to prevent worsening symptoms, mitigate what's already going on, and trying to live the day in the best health possible. This means committing to, at the very minimum, two hours a day of treatments, consisting of a breathing machine with a vest, a nebulizer with several separate inhaled medications, and various pills and liquid forms of medication throughout the day. And that's the healthy side of CF. Most kids spend many weeks – even months – a year in the hospital, be it for antibiotic infusions known in the CF community as "tune-ups," or for infections, exacerbations, or pancreatic insufficiency.

For this and other various reasons, CF kids are often homeschooled.

For a child with CF on the healthier side, going to school means waking up extra early to get at least an hour of treatment in, along with a full, high-calorie, high-fat breakfast. This is only possible if they haven't been up all night coughing.

As mentioned earlier, after nights like this I sometimes couldn't bring myself to wake GR at 5:30 a.m. when she had finally fallen asleep around 4. I knew she'd be exhausted and likely have an even rougher day or evening if she didn't get rest. Being late for school definitely seemed the better option.

Other mornings, she would wake up in so much stomach pain that it required extra time in the bathroom to try to move stuff through her little body that hadn't been properly digested or was causing a blockage or distension. This meant she wouldn't be able to eat before school, thus losing an opportunity for more caloric intake.

I always packed her lunch. It would consist of several high-calorie and high-fat options that were also healthy, fibrous, and comfortably digestible. This was a method of finding her favorite foods, finding how to add calories to those foods, and determining what mood her body would be in for the day in order to be able to digest the foods, as she needed to eat all day in order to get in the prescribed 5,000 calories. This also meant closely monitoring her enzyme intake throughout the day, be it snack time, lunchtime, or any time she drank something other than water. If the correct dosage wasn't delivered before each intake, it would result in further abdominal issues that would impact the rest of the day, the evening, and possibly the next morning.

I knew kindergarten would involve a slightly stricter protocol than preschool or nursery school, where I could bring GR late or keep her home altogether if she was having a rough morning. I decided early on that I would volunteer to be a classroom mom, because I wanted to be helpful but also to keep an eye on Grace-Rose and make sure she was taking the proper medication before snacks or lunch. I also needed to make sure she was always drinking water. I had learned to add mint to the water to help with digestion and to give her Gatorade with higher sodium. Her class had PE outside, and with temperatures sometimes reaching the nineties she would get significantly dehydrated and severe headaches. Drinking water with salt tablets, although she didn't like it, was recommended for CF kids to help replenish salt as well as remind them to drink more. This is common in those with Cystic Fibrosis because they don't retain salt in the cells. We were always **adding salt** to everything!

Her lunches might include all of the following: sliced apples, cucumbers, a peanut butter sandwich, beans and rice (with an invisible high-calorie powder added), cheese pizza with extra cheese, shredded chicken, broccoli florets, highly salted potato chips, chocolate chip chewy granola bar, cheese stick, graham crackers, and a brownie. Baggies would be labeled with the amount of "jellybeans" she had to take with each one. (She would refer to her enzymes as jellybeans if friends asked what she was taking.)

This way, I could see what was eaten, if anything, and automatically know how her stomach was feeling that day and what she would need for afternoon snack and dinner in order to get those calories in, as well as the right amount of fiber. The lunch boxes would be refrigerated or kept cold so that no food would go to waste. On special occasions she would get a sushi burger – crispy rice patties with spicy tuna or salmon in the middle and sliced avocado – or a cut roll. Sushi was her favorite and had been ever since she was little, when we used to pick it up on the way home from the Hollywood YMCA. The Y was on the other side of the hill in Hollywood and Shintaro, a small sushi spot on Franklin Avenue, was halfway home. We'd pick up a little snack for GR to eat while she was waiting for me to fix dinner. She called it "Kathy sushi" because Kathy was the hostess who adored her. Kathy would welcome her with a small sake pitcher and cup filled with "Sprine-apple", a favorite concoction that GR had created: Sprite and Pineapple. This was always her treat when we went out to eat. We never had soda at home.

Kathy would deliver this "sake," then GR would play with the rock garden while we waited for a special roll or the garlic green beans to take home. She particularly liked the tobiko rolls – she always asked for extra tobiko – and the chef would sometimes deliver a roll wrapped on top of a chopstick that he called a special sushi lollipop. I believe her love for it may in part be that it was easy on her digestive system. It was also good because the tobiko had a higher sodium content.

Lucky for us, our Studio City neighborhood is known as "sushi-row," with some of LA's best sushi restaurants. There would be no shortage of her favorites to choose from.

* * *

I recall walking out of school after lunch one day and running into one of the other moms. "Leah," she said, "the moms want to know what you put in GR's lunch each day. Apparently, all the kids come home talking about it."

"I basically dump the fridge in there!" I replied jokingly, then added that it was for medical reasons.

Needless to say, each day was a journey that GR had to navigate carefully and strategically. We were fortunate enough to live within walking distance of school and took full advantage of it. I'd always enjoyed a morning walk, and our walks to school were a great way to relieve any pent-up stress or anxiousness from the morning. The walk was meant to be either meditative or communicative, based on our moods.

Sometimes we started with GR on her scooter (we'd tried a skateboard, but that didn't seem to stick), which got us there quicker and I could lightly jog to keep up. This became a much more fun and efficient way to get to school, especially if we were running late. We decked the scooter out with accessories, including a cup holder so I could grab my iced coffee either to or from the route, depending on time.

I cherished that time together each morning. I recall getting emotional on our final walk to the elementary school when GR was in the fifth grade. Our morning routine would end, I thought, as I held her hand, no longer little, and realized how grown up she seemed.

However, at this point, GR was starting kindergarten, we still had several years of walks in our future, and we were starting to get to know our new community. Most of the moms were from Los Angeles or had lived here for a long time. Several had sent their kids to preschools nearby and had already bonded with other children and their parents. Yet, we were warmly welcomed, and it felt comforting.

When it came time for the kindergarten picnic, Grace-Rose and I were excited to have a fun day with our new friends at Beaman Park. It was a Saturday morning, and as usual on the weekends we slept a little bit late, though never very late because of treatments. I noticed this particular morning that GR was feeling more stomach pain than usual. However, she would never let CF dampen her anticipated plans. She would power through. She'd rarely complain until after an event or an occasion. Sometimes this would make symptoms worsen because we'd waited too long to start treating them. She just didn't want anything to interfere with "life."

She insisted on going to the picnic. I tried feeding her breakfast, to no avail, which was sometimes the case because of her stomach pains. This only meant I was going to have to get more calories into her in the remaining hours of the day, of which never seemed like enough. I also realized she hadn't gone to the bathroom or really eaten since earlier the previous day. I was aware but not too concerned, and we headed off to the picnic. GR ran around, making new friends and really enjoying herself. I went over to bring her some pills and a slice of pizza, but she wouldn't touch it. Now we were halfway through the day without her having consumed a single calorie, and yes, the fact that I had to think about food and calories all day long was extremely tedious.

I'd always enjoyed exercise, sports, working out, and eating healthy, and now everything I had ever been taught about nutritious food was basically the opposite of what I was supposed to be teaching my child. In fact, CF kids and their parents would often joke that at least they got to eat whatever and whenever they wanted without worrying about gaining weight. I mean, what young girl is told that a milkshake with ice cream, peanut butter, extra fudge, and whipped cream right before bed is HEALTHY?

Doctors would encourage me to take her to get fast food due to its high fat and calorie content. Add extra cheese to her pizza, bacon to her hamburger, and eat fried food. I had always preferred farmers markets and home-cooked meals. We rarely ate fast food, so that wasn't where we gravitated to for calories and fat.

They would prescribe powdered calories that would disappear in her food. I'd add it to milkshakes, dinners, drinks, her favorite dishes like halibut over shredded cabbage – really anything I could prepare as a healthy dining option. I didn't want my child just having fast food while I was eating a salad. I wanted us both to eat healthy. I wanted us to eat together; mealtimes were my favorite. It was an easy way to communicate and learn so much about her day, her feelings, just simple conversation. I knew if I was feeding her something but not eating it myself, she would be more hesitant to eat it. The most important thing for me was to remember to label the leftovers that had the extra, invisible "hidden calories."

* * *

On this particular day at the park, all seemed to be going well, other than the fact that she hadn't had any food. Suddenly, she came up to me almost doubled over in stomach pain and said we needed to leave. At this point I was reminded that not only had she not eaten since early evening the night before which to a regular person would be equivalent to days without food, but she also still hadn't gone to the bathroom.

"Feel my tummy," she said, and when I did it felt like a huge rock was lodged inside. We had never had these complications before, and not knowing what else to do, I decided to take her to the ER. We went to Providence St Joe's Hospital in Burbank, which was the closest option. The doctors were perplexed by what they saw on her scans and x-rays. When I described her symptoms, they thought she needed to have an emergency appendectomy – until I said that I thought it may be related to the CF. They were not educated enough around this disease because at the time there were not as many adults with CF, let alone adult care centers for people with it. They needed to send us to a Children's Hospital.

GR had been going to CF clinics at Cedars Sinai, which the preschool mom had recommended, but when her pulmonary doctor left he sent us to Children's Hospital in Long Beach. This was where his team had been transferred. So we were not familiar with Children's Hospital LA. We rode in an ambulance – my first time, but unfortunately not my last – to CHLA. We spent the first night running tests and under observation until the pulmonary team arrived the next morning to wake us. This is when they told us there was a blockage in her intestines, similar to the one she'd been born with. It looked like a baseball was protruding from her stomach. My concern was this would lead to another surgery, which seemed all too soon for my little four-and-a-half-year-old. However, the doctors and nurses said we could try using laxatives, saline waters, and enemas to see if we could dislodge the blockage. She wasn't allowed to consume anything other than the saline solution. They would use an IV drip to keep her hydrated. She would lose weight. I would take small breaks to hide in the hallways or downstairs in order to have some crackers or a granola bar. I didn't want to eat in front of her because I knew she was starving, but I also didn't want to leave her. I slept by her side in the hospital – something I was used to because we shared a bed, though I wasn't used to being woken up all night for assessments and vitals.

During the stay, we had visitors – friends and family. They brought gifts, flowers, toys, even cute little outfits. This was our first hospitalization, and from what I was being told by all the nurses, certainly not our last. They were trying to prepare me for the inevitable. We were actually in the wing of the hospital that treated only CF patients, because they spent so much time there. I was saddened and overwhelmed by this notion but determined that this would not be our case.

GR had been sent home with kindergarten homework, but I didn't like the idea of requiring her to do it while in the hospital. It just felt cruel. It was the same way I felt about treatments. I didn't want GR making negative associations between medical issues and school. Of course, if she wanted to work on something school-related, she could. I just didn't want it to be mandatory. Besides, she needed something to do other than homework, and neither of us watched much TV. I was raised without a TV and didn't seem to mind. It inspired me and my siblings to be active, play sports, play outside with friends, or read. I had a similar rule with GR. No TV on the weeknights, just a few windows of viewing on the weekends, particularly with treatments. This would sometimes result in her doing an extra treatment, by choice.

GR did enjoy cartoons, but we certainly weren't going to spend the entire day in the hospital watching them. In order to stay busy, we found coloring books, which she enjoyed. She was also very observant of what was going on around her, and noticed that the nurses came in and out throughout the day, twenty-four hours a day. She didn't think they ever went home to sleep.

At one point during this hospital stay she said, "Mom, I think these nurses need a cupcake!" She thought a treat, and some sugar for all their hard work, was what they needed to help get them through the night. When we were being discharged ten days later, she told her "saltwater nurse "– the nickname she gave to the nurse who kept forcing her to drink this liquid – that she would remember to bring her some cupcakes. The nurse then turned to her and said, "Okay, thank you, you'll probably be back soon."

In that moment, it took everything in me to hold it together. The thought of this becoming a regular and potentially worsening situation terrified me.

We would then transfer to CHLA, which had some of the best pulmonary doctors. We appreciated the care as well as the convenience, it was much closer than Long Beach.

That visit was in early September. For her birthday, which is November 27th, right around Thanksgiving, we thought it would be a nice gesture to make coloring books for the kids in the hospital. It would also become one of our creative outlets. GR would come up with a cute theme, then either draw images for kids to color or print pages from books she liked in black and white. These homemade books always included a sweet, encouraging note and crayons from GR to the patient. This became a yearly tradition and we would deliver the coloring books the week of Thanksgiving, along with cupcakes for the nurses. It was our way of showing gratitude to them and, even more so, for having avoided any recent hospital stays.

California Burrito

GR loved this high-calorie burrito from a local taco stand near our home in L.A.

Carne Asada, guacamole, and french fries

Ingredients

For the Burrito:

- 1 lb. carne asada (grilled or cooked steak), cut into thin strips or small cubes
- 1 large flour tortilla (12 inches or larger) per burrito
- 1 cup shredded Mexican cheese blend or cheddar cheese
- 1/2 cup guacamole (store-bought or homemade)
- 1/2 cup sour cream
- 1/2 cup pico de gallo or salsa
- 1-2 large russet potatoes (for fresh French fries) or use frozen French fries
- Salt, to taste
- Vegetable oil (for frying or baking fries)

For the Carne Asada Marinade (optional):

- 1/4 cup soy sauce
- 1/4 cup lime juice (about 2-3 limes)
- 2 tbsp olive oil
- 2 cloves garlic, minced
- 1/2 tsp cumin powder
- 1/2 tsp chili powder
- Salt and pepper to taste

Instructions

Step 1: Prepare the Carne Asada

1. Marinate the Steak (Optional): Combine soy sauce, lime juice, olive oil, garlic, cumin, chili powder, salt, and pepper in a bowl. Add the steak, cover, and let it marinate in the fridge for 30 minutes to 1 hour for extra flavor.

2. Cook the Steak: Grill or pan-sear the carne asada over medium-high heat for 3-4 minutes per side (or until it reaches your desired level of doneness). Let it rest for a few minutes before slicing into thin strips or small cubes.

Step 2: Prepare the French Fries

1. If Using Fresh Potatoes: Peel and cut potatoes into thin, even sticks. Soak them in water for 15 minutes to remove starch, then pat dry.

2. Fry the Fries: Heat vegetable oil in a large pan or pot to 350°F (175°C). Fry the potatoes in small batches for about 5-7 minutes, or until golden and crispy. Remove, drain on paper towels, and season with salt. Alternatively, you can bake or air-fry the French fries if preferred.

Step 3: Assemble the Burrito

1. Warm the Tortilla: Heat the tortilla in a pan or microwave briefly to make it soft and pliable.

2. Layer the Ingredients: On the center of the tortilla, layer carne asada, cheese, guacamole, sour cream, pico de gallo or salsa, and a generous handful of French fries.

3. Wrap It Up: Fold the sides of the tortilla inward and roll up tightly from the bottom. If needed, wrap it in foil to hold it together.

Step 4: Toast the Burrito (Optional)

1. Toast for Extra Flavor: Heat a skillet over medium heat and toast the burrito for 1-2 minutes per side, until lightly golden and crispy.

* For extra seasoning, sprinkle Mexican sea salt on the fries before assembly

EIGHT

TIA LEAH CAMP – THE PHONE CALL

Figuring out summer camp was always a challenge. Sleepaway camp was out of the question because I couldn't trust anyone else with GR's treatments and medications. I knew each summer we would return to New Orleans for at least a month to visit friends and family, and in fact part of me still thought we might move back in the near future. We were also still hosting her summer fundraisers in NOLA, so this gave me time to plan the events while GR would attend a day camp.

I would utilize the time to find sponsors and auction donors; determine the theme, location, food and beverage, fashion, models, clothes, and rentals; and handle PR and promotions – securing spots on news shows, or getting articles, and interviews. I loved the work, and it was an enjoyable topic of conversation with GR, making the two or three hours she was hooked up to her treatments each day more tolerable. Everything needed to be approved by her as she was "the host" and very opinionated.

Since my clothing line was being sold either online or at in-person events such as trunk shows and hosted house parties, I was allowed more flexibility. As a sole, full-time caregiver, flexibility was the only way I was going to be able to do all of this. It certainly came with some financial insecurities but I couldn't determine a better alternative. Hoping for some guidance, I had asked our CF community several times if they knew of any other single CF parent who had no co-parenting assistance, financially or physically. They couldn't find anyone, so I was left to figure this out on my own.

When we got to New Orleans, we always stayed downtown in the Warehouse District — a fun and convenient part of town. It was also relatively close to where I grew up, Uptown, a quick streetcar ride down St. Charles Avenue. The city is small, much smaller than Los Angeles, and fairly easy to navigate. We tried various random camps, such as Zoo Camp, however, the heat and mosquitoes were too much for GR. She would end camp severely dehydrated and full of welts because mosquitoes loved her salty skin. The JCC had a sports camp, but the heat was still a factor; plus, while sports were fun we'd come to realize they really weren't her thing.

One of the camps GR really enjoyed was the nearby Contemporary Arts Center (CAC) camp. With the exception of one summer fashion camp at the Ogden Museum, the CAC camp became her routine. We loved that it incorporated theater, art, and cooking which were all things we thoroughly enjoyed. Plus, its close proximity allowed me to pop in and check on her whenever necessary.

The camp was sponsored by the Emeril Lagasse Foundation, and at the culmination of each week there would be a performance, an art exhibit, and a creative culinary experience all based on the week's theme. Every Friday the parents would gather in the auditorium to watch a show. One silly theme I remember was "local seafood and gumbo." The kids sang Cajun songs, while dressed in different seafood costumes, then jumped into a large pot as others danced around. Honestly, I think it was all very amusing for GR as it was such a departure from the theater shows she was participating in, in Los Angeles. I would often joke and call her my "little Creole Valley girl."

Once the performance was over, we'd all get to observe the kids' art, which adorned the walls of the museum, and the tables full of food and desserts they created to match the theme. After savoring this culinary delight, GR and I would stroll back to the condo for some pool time. Later, we'd visit a refreshing sno-ball stand before wrapping up the day with medical treatments and event planning.

Back in California, my mother had started her own tradition: every summer she took GR and my sister's kids, Zander and Jasper, to the Hotel Del Coronado, located on Coronado, a small island off San Diego. Built in 1888, "The Del" is one of the oldest hotels in California and has a rich history that includes the filming of "Some *Like It Hot*" *with* Marilyn Monroe. It was also where L. Frank Baum wrote much of "*The Wizard of Oz.*" (It was recently acquired by the Hilton group and while it has been updated it maintains the original aesthetic.) The kids always looked forward to this trip, and I went with them to make sure GR was doing her daily treatments and taking all her meds.

We would take the train from Union Station in Downtown LA to Santa Fe station in Downtown San Diego. A journey we all enjoyed, and I appreciated not having to drive. Mom always reserved business class seats so we'd be assured a table and "free snacks." Once we arrived, we would take either a ferry or a car ride over to the island. GR and her cousins spent their days between the pool and the ocean, alternating between bodyboarding or some water sport and surrey rides — the large bikes that four people can pedal. Visits to MooTime Creamery, the ice cream and candy shop, was a traditional activity, as well as at least one morning of room service and one morning at the extensive breakfast buffet. We'd typically spend a day at the San Diego Zoo as well. The trip would end with a visit to the gift shop for a small token as a vacation memory.

This still left me with at least a month of summer to plan for camp or activities. My sister was also looking for different camp options for her boys. That's when I came up with the concept of "Tia Leah Camp." Zander and Jasper were the closest thing GR had to siblings, and since we had spent so much time together at Sunday family dinners and such, I knew I'd be able to care for the three of them. The name, Tia Leah, was what the boys always called me, a nod to GR's Cuban side.

I proposed the idea of Tia Leah Camp to my sister, knowing she'd be getting a better deal with me at the helm than at the expensive day camps where she usually enrolled them.

Still, to convince her to pay me for the camp, I needed to show her that it would be structured, with a scheduled itinerary. I came up with a plan to have a different theme each day, such as Art, Sports, Cooking, Water Activities, Adventure Day, and so on. The itinerary would then be created around the theme.

On Water Activities days we would go to the beach or find different pools around the city, sometimes they even had DJ's; on Adventure Days we'd discover different hikes to waterfalls and creeks or I'd let them choose something of interest, like a silly Hollywood attraction. Museum Days would consist of visiting a museum of their choice and then creating a piece of artwork inspired by the exhibits. Sports Days could be anything from tennis to mini-golf or basketball. We'd play the sport, run obstacle courses, or do some 'made-up' activity involving the sport, then either watch something related to it or learn about a famous player. Cooking Days would include coming up with a dinner concept and going shopping, be it to an ethnic marketplace, a regular grocery store, a farmers market and, on some occasions, a farm. Once, we went to a café owned and operated by a friend of mine; who graciously agreed to let us come and learn some cooking techniques in the kitchen. When we got home, we'd cook a meal for everyone to enjoy, based on whatever the excursion or theme was.

My sister was sold, and Tia Leah Camp began. It was great fun for all of us – and it provided me with a different way to keep GR occupied while also managing her healthcare.

* * *

Some of the most common lung bacteria that can grow in a CF person's lungs and worsen their function are Pseudomonas (pseudomonas aeruginosa) Staph (staphylococcus aureus) MRSA (methicillin-resistant staphylococcus aureus), and B. Cepacia (burkholderia cepacia complex.

A healthy adult or child can typically fight off these bacteria, but for a person with CF, they can cause severe, life-threatening infections that may ultimately require a lung transplant. *B. cepacia*, in particular, leads to a more rapid decline in lung function, primarily due to its resistance to antibiotics.

If one of these bacteria becomes present, additional inhaled antibiotics become part of the already rigorous daily protocol. Once started, it's difficult to wean someone off of them; however, doctors don't want the patients to become immune to the antibiotics because these infections can take over the lungs.

CF patients have to practice isolation in clinics and doctors are fully protected during visitations, due to these highly contagious infections and to avoid cross-contamination.

Moreover, CF patients are always cautioned to practice the six-feet-apart rule or, better yet, never come in contact with one another. This is why CF patients didn't have strong support groups or communities. It's also why parents didn't have strong support groups or communities. It's very difficult to befriend a parent of someone with CF when your children, who have so much in common, can never meet or play together. It has since changed a bit with social media and technology.

I recall seeing one mom in the pulmonary clinic with her daughter; the girl was around the same age as GR and the mom was in obvious distress. I wanted to go hug her, tell her we could be friends, our daughters could be friends, we could support one another. But I knew I couldn't; she knew we couldn't. We just looked at each other with a heaviness of heart.

It is very common for children who become infected with lung bacteria to spend several weeks at a time in the hospital, taking IV antibiotics because the daily inhaled antibiotics aren't strong enough. This is known in the CF community as "regular tune-ups" to try to fight the bacteria. It is one of the reasons the nurses at our first hospital visit kept telling us she would "see us soon."

In fact, when we started kindergarten, one of the other room mothers I had befriended happened to be close to a CF mom and offered to introduce us. She mentioned that the family was very involved with our local Los Angeles CF Foundation and might have some helpful advice.

I went to the Beverly Hills home of this woman, whose name is Diane, to meet with her and a director from the CF Foundation. Diane's daughter, Mallory, was fourteen years old at the time. She was playing volleyball at Beverly Hills HS and doing well. However, she had recently contracted *B. cepacia*. I went home to shower before picking up Grace-Rose from school, just in case I had been exposed. At the time, I was still relatively new to the disease and didn't fully understand all the risks and protocols.

For many years, we would keep a photo of the tall, blond, athletic Mallory on our fridge as an inspiration. We followed and supported one another from afar. The B. Cepacia eventually landed Mallory on the transplant list, her health rapidly declining as she waited for a new set of lungs. She finally received them, only to succumb to an infection. Mallory was a prolific writer and had journaled detailed accounts of her life, including her heartbreaking struggles with CF, and her fear of dying. She had instructed her mother to compile these accounts and release them as a memoir titled *Salt in My Soul – An Unfinished Life* – should she not survive. We were heartbroken to learn of her passing just one month post transplant. Her memoir was later adapted into a documentary, painting a vivid portrait of her beautiful life intertwined with ongoing fears and health decline.

* * *

One Sports Day at Tia Leah Camp, we were doing tennis drills at Beaman Park. It was part relay race, part obstacle course; they would have to pick up one of the tennis balls that I had stationed all over the court with the aim of hitting it into a specific square, then run across the court and do the same on the other side. We took turns timing each kid. It was a silly deviation from a traditional game.

I remember this day because it came right after Grace-Rose had a CF clinic. These clinics were held quarterly, lasted almost the entire day, and were quite exhausting. They began with a nurse taking vitals, most importantly height and weight — we always prayed for weight gain. GR would then proceed into what looked like a clear telephone booth, hook up to a breathing apparatus that was connected to a computer, and start doing different breathing tests called pulmonary function tests, or PFTs. This would measure her lung function and lung capacity, including any decline.

For CF people, declining lung function is inevitable; all the treatments they do are to help slow it down. For the younger patients, the tests would consist of cartoons on the screen, where they could choose to try to blow out all the candles on a cake or send Icarus to the sun. These were meant to incentivize them to breathe as hard as they possibly could while pushing air out of their lungs. PFTs were always nerve-racking for me because I could see the numbers on the computer, but I tried to remain as stoic as possible. I knew GR could read my energy, and she had maintained that my calming voice soothed her. I reminded myself of that whenever I was in her presence, so as not to scare her. I would watch as her lung function slowly declined, and it took all I had to hold back tears.

With every PFT, I would think, *How much more will they drop? How will this affect her breathing? How will this affect her treatments? How will this affect future increasing hospitalizations? How would this affect, ultimately, longevity?*

After PFTs, we would go back into our isolated room and wait for the next specialist to come in. Some days, when these waits were longer than usual, we would have to find silly ways to occupy our time. Playing Simon Says was one of them. No cellular devices were allowed in the rooms; nor was food or drink, but I would often sneak food in so GR wouldn't miss out on crucial caloric intake during these long days.

The next visit would be a dietician, who continually tried to convince me to allow a G-tube to be surgically inserted into her belly, due to her lack of weight gain and growth. We would then listen as the nutritionist went over all the fatty, high-calorie foods she should be eating to reach five thousand calories a day. Then the pharmacist would come in to go over all of her medications, the dosages, how they were working, and if any of them needed to be increased. Determining this in accordance with her pancreatic insufficiency would be an ongoing science experiment. Next was a visit from the pulmonologist.

They would start by checking her fingertips first, because that's how they could determine whether the lungs were being further compromised. People with CF tend to have clubbing fingertips and if they become more prominent it could be due to a lack of oxygen. The doctor would then check her belly for any distension or blockage and, finally, listen to the lungs for any rattling or distressed breathing. The PFTs were also reviewed and we'd discuss the numbers and what they meant. I only recall losing it two times in the clinic. The first was when her doctor came in and was very concerned about her PFTs.

This particular visit and day had been difficult to begin with and I had just hit an emotional wall. The doctor came in and asked how I was doing. At this simple, well-meaning question, I burst into tears. Not knowing how to handle this reaction, she said, "I'm going to get the social worker."

When she left the room, I ran into the bathroom, splashed cold water on my face, and somehow managed to stop the tears. By the time the social worker arrived, I apologized for rushing her in, but what I truly felt sorry for was that GR had witnessed my breakdown. She already had enough in her life to cause anxiety, and I never wanted to add to that by showing my own fear. I always aimed to appear positive and calm, and I felt deeply disappointed in myself for not having done so.

The second breakdown was much later, when I was worried about my mother's health. I had been taking care of both of them full-time and, once again, was at my emotional limit. When our favorite nurse came in to check on us and asked how I was doing, I lost it. She thoughtfully pulled me into an empty room and allowed me to cry. Clearly, people asking me how I was doing was an emotional trigger.

After the pulmonologist left, we would be visited by a social worker to discuss any mental health concerns. Once GR turned twelve, the social worker began speaking to her alone, the purpose being to find out if there was anything GR felt she couldn't discuss with me – for example, suicidal thoughts, drug and alcohol use, sexual activity or pregnancy, and so on.

Grace-Rose would always tell the social worker that it was fine for me to stay, but since the social worker insisted, I would step out to grab a coffee. Then, once the social worker had left, GR would tell me everything they'd talked about. The clinic would end with a nurse coming in with discharge papers, notes, and a swab for GR's throat to test for any of the noted bacteria. Typically, CF patients could easily cough up mucus, but this wasn't the case for GR. She needed to be swabbed.

On this particular day, the day after clinic, we were on the tennis courts when my phone started ringing. I wasn't too concerned when I saw that it was the doctor. She was no doubt calling with the results of the swab, and they had always been negative. Instead, the doctor told me it had come back positive for pseudomonas.

Grace-Rose was still on the court, but Zander, who was sitting next to me, asked if I was okay. I'm certain he sensed my alarm.

"Not really," I said, "but I will be. Let's go home now."

I wasn't quite sure how to share this news with Grace-Rose, but I knew I needed to soon. We would now have to add more medications and inhaled antibiotics to her already rigorous regimen.

More time out of her youthful childhood.

Creole Jambalaya

Recipe from our friend and chef Steve Price of AMDA cafe in Hollywood, (*adapted* from chef Frank Brigtsen's recipe of Brigtsen's Restaurant in New Orleans.)

Serves 8
Ingredients:

- Proteins & Broth:
  - 2 lb. medium shrimp, peeled (reserve heads and shells)
  - 1 lb. Andouille or smoked pork sausage (or kielbasa), cut into ¼" rounds
  - 1 lb. chicken thigh meat, cut into ½" pieces
  - 3 cups chicken broth, canned or homemade

1.
- Vegetables:
  - 3 medium red bell peppers, finely diced
  - 3 medium green bell peppers, finely diced
  - 1 bunch celery, finely diced
  - 6 medium yellow onions, finely diced
  - 6 cloves garlic, minced
  - 4 green onions, thinly sliced (for garnish)

2.
- Spices & Seasoning:
  - 3 bay leaves
  - 1 15 oz can crushed tomatoes
  - 1 ½ tbsp kosher salt
  - ½ tsp black pepper
  - ¼ tsp white pepper

- ¼ tsp cayenne pepper
- ¼ tsp ground turmeric
- 1 tsp dried oregano
- ½ tsp dried basil
- ½ tsp smoked paprika
- 1 tbsp Worcestershire sauce
- Grains:
  - 3 cups basmati or long-grain white rice

Instructions:

1. Prep and Caramelize Vegetables:
   - Preheat the oven to 400°F.
   - Combine diced bell peppers, celery, and onions. Reserve half for later.
   - In a large Dutch oven, heat olive oil over medium-low heat. Add half of the pepper, celery, and onion mixture, and caramelize for about 25 minutes, stirring occasionally.

2. Make Shrimp Stock:
   - In a saucepan, combine the reserved shrimp heads and shells with chicken broth.
   - Bring to a boil, then reduce to a simmer for 20 minutes. Strain the broth to remove solids.
   - Stir in crushed tomatoes and bring the mixture back to a simmer.

3. Brown the Sausage:
   - On a baking sheet, roast the sausage rounds in the oven for about 12 minutes until browned in spots.

4. Build the Jambalaya Base:
   - Add the remaining onion, pepper, and celery mixture to the caramelized vegetables in the Dutch oven. Stir in garlic and cook until fragrant.
   - Mix in bay leaves, spices, and herbs. Cook for 2-3 minutes until the spices bloom.
   - Stir in the chicken pieces and cook until they lose their raw color.

5. Add Rice and Stock:
   - Stir the rice into the vegetable and chicken mixture, cooking until the rice turns opaque white.
   - Add the browned sausage along with any rendered fat, followed by the simmering tomato-chicken broth.
   - Bring the pot to a hard boil. Taste the broth—it should be slightly salty to account for the rice absorption.

6. Cook and Bake:
   - Stir in the shrimp and bring everything back to a hard boil.
   - Cover the pot and transfer to the oven. Bake for 10 minutes at 400°F, then reduce heat to 375°F and cook for another 15-20 minutes.

7. Rest and Serve:
   - Remove the pot from the oven and let it sit, covered, for 5 minutes.
   - Fluff the jambalaya with a fork and garnish with sliced green onions.

* Top with a little Creole sea salt

NINE

SECOND GRADE – TWICE

I'd always been one to have a spiritual or self-help book on my reading list. *How to Talk So Kids Will Listen and Listen So Kids Will Talk*, by Adele Faber and Elaine Mazlish, was recommended to me as a good book to read while raising a child. I found this to be true, and the book had been on my nightstand for quite a while. Though GR and I shared a bedroom, I never thought much about the books I put there... until she learned to read.

One day, out of the blue, she asked me if I had that book because she had done something wrong.

"Oh no, love," I said, "It's quite the opposite, I am reading this book to try to help me be the best parent to you that I can possibly be."

There was one chapter in the book that stuck with me, about how anxiety and stress in children are exactly as they are in us as adults. If there's something upsetting or stressful for them, we shouldn't "belittle it" by saying something such as, "Oh, it's not a big deal that you left your stuff at school, we can just pick it up tomorrow," or "Don't worry about that little cut on your knee, it will heal quickly." It's more helpful if you really try to understand how sad or stressful a situation may be for them. It may feel big to them, because it is. They are young and inexperienced with difficult situations, so the goal is to respond in a way that gives them a sense of agency. First, listen and give their concern the attention it deserves. Then, if possible, try to help them get to a resolution. I also really resonated with the idea of listening first, being fully present, and then feeling as though GR was really listening to me when I was talking.

* * *

Mealtimes were very special; they were a time of communication and connection, just like when I was growing up. I had even designated one night a month as a special "date night," when GR and I would get dressed up, go somewhere fancy, and just chit-chat. My mother was back and forth between L.A. and New Orleans and lived with us half the time, so most dinners were the three of us. When she was back in New Orleans, GR and I would pick a new spot to try. There was something about just the two of us, having this special evening. I still have several drawings from restaurants that offered her a set of crayons and paper menus to color on while we were talking and waiting for food. My favorite is from Pastis, where we ate on a trip to New York City, framed on the back of their menu.

What mattered most to me is that she felt seen and heard. This, I've since learned, is most important for cultivating confidence and security in young children, giving them the best chance for a successful future.

* * *

After almost forty years of marriage, my parents announced that they were getting a divorce. My father had moved back to Massachusetts after Hurricane Katrina and was getting remarried. My mother didn't take it very well, and those emotions often came up during dinnertime conversations. When this happened, I would excuse GR early and ask her to go do her treatment in the bedroom. While I understood Mom's anger and sadness, I didn't want my daughter to be exposed to the negative energy. She was too young to understand these kinds of situations, and

I didn't want her to get the idea that men disappearing from her life was a pattern.

GR and I had always had open conversations about her father. I was never afraid to tell her anything about our relationship or how we met, but it would confuse her as to why he was no longer around. Frankly, it confused me too. I always wanted her to know she was meant to be here and created from a place of love. This was true. I didn't need to tell her anything bad; Eli's actions would speak for themselves. When we visited New York City, I would show her where we first met and places we used to play basketball or go out to eat. I wanted her to know the whole story. I wanted her to know about the relationship. However, the dialogue would have to match her maturity level in order to fully comprehend it.

The topic didn't come up often. But it would always be a conversation on Father's Day, mostly because they were making cards at school, and she wasn't sure who to create hers for. She finally just started making the cards for me, because I was both. I think GR actually found it funny, particularly when other students would comment as if she didn't know which day it was. A sense of humor has always been one of GR's favorite qualities about herself. Mine too.

When the discussion of her absentee father did come up at dinner, I would speak openly about it.

I remember when she was very young and couldn't write words yet, she was sitting at her little desk in the corner of the living room. She seemed to be ferociously scribbling something on paper. When I asked what she was working on she whipped around and said, "I'm writing a 'per-scription' for my daddy's head." I had explained to her that he had "problems with his head" and that's why he wasn't around. I figured that was the best way to describe his issues and actions to a three-year-old. Since she had witnessed her doctors writing prescriptions for all her ailments, she assumed this was just what you did if something's wrong with your body.

During one dinner conversation, when we were speculating as to where her father might be, GR excitedly blurted out, "I have a great idea! We can go find him at Abuela's house in New York!" We knew where his mother lived and were aware that he sometimes visited her. "And," she continued, "we can tell him we're taking him to a Taylor Swith concert."

I didn't want to interrupt her grandiose idea to tell her that it was, in fact, Swift.

Considering her age, GR made a pretty astute assumption that someone could be swayed by these tickets, especially since Taylor Swift had recently become incredibly popular.

"Okay," I said, "and then what?"

She replied as if it was so obvious. "Then we take him outside and instead of turning right, we turn left and drive him right to the hospital and drop him off so they can fix his head!" For whatever reason she had it in her mind that the concert was in one direction and the hospital was in the opposite.

Her plan was adorable, but beneath it was a desperation that made me so sad for her, for both of us. If only he could see how amazing she was and how little we needed from him in return. She was always thinking of ways to try to fix his head. Much later, when she was mature enough to understand, I'd explain that his real issues were commitment and responsibility – two of the most crucial attributes for being a parent.

When Eli disappeared, I'd made it a point to connect with his older daughter, Alisa, who lived in New York and was ten years older than GR. Though he ultimately had abandoned her too, she'd had a longer relationship with him and knew about GR. I had been in contact with Alisa's mother, and when we visited New York I made sure to get the girls together. Alisa's mother was African American and there was no CF gene in her family. I wanted it to be abundantly clear to both of them that his leaving had nothing to do with their ethnicity, where they lived, or any health issues they may have. It had nothing to do with them and everything to do with him.

GR was in second grade when the TV show *Glee* came out. She was not allowed to watch TV on weeknights; as mentioned, I had grown up without a TV and found it beneficial. Glee was an exception. It was a musical show and felt similar to the movie *High School Musical*, which GR had been obsessed with. She had such a huge crush on Zac Efron after HSM and referred to him as "So mashy." When I asked her what that meant exactly, she said "Oh you know, when you see a cute boy it's that feeling you get inside, like a mashed potato." Impressed and amused by the association, from then on I joined GR in referring to cute boys we saw as "so mashy." Zac Efron remained the epitome of 'mashiness,' so it was incredibly special when, during the dinner celebrating her seventh birthday, a gift arrived at the door. It was a framed picture of him with the inscription, 'To Grace-Rose, all my love... Zac.' Our neighbor and good friend, Donal, who was aware of GR's crush and happened to be working on a movie with Zac, had it delivered. Witnessing GR's expression upon opening the gift, it seemed all her birthday wishes had been fulfilled.

Seeing that *Glee* truly excited her as well, I created a fun ritual around it. On Tuesdays, we would walk to a nearby favorite sushi spot, grab takeout, and watch the show together. Sushi-Glee night was something to look forward to each week and furthered her passion for singing, dancing, and acting.

Her serious interest in musical theater started right before kindergarten. Her first performance was at my old school in New Orleans, Sacred Heart. I thoroughly enjoyed my experience there before I transferred to Ben Franklin for high school. I wanted her to have a connection to where I spent my youth. The play was *Seussical the Musical* and GR was a "Who" in Whoville. She was hooked.

At Carpenter, her elementary school, she quickly became engaged in the musical theater community. By second grade, she was already in her third production. I often volunteered in the wardrobe department or wherever needed in order to help offset some of the costs of these expensive extracurriculars. She was the youngest in her second-grade class. I was well aware of this when she was leaving preschool, but they insisted that she was ready.

She has always loved school, and "teaching school" on "the weekends off," as she would say, was one of her favorite things to do. In fact, Sunday family dinners gave her the opportunity to teach her cousins. She would prepare all weekend for it, setting up a mock classroom and some version of a whiteboard, either our glass window or dry erase calendar. To get GR to attend mass, Mimi (as the grandkids referred to my mom) would bribe her with a trip to the 99-cent store after. GR loved going to the 99-cent store because she could pick up more teaching supplies and even grab random trinkets for her "treasure box." That's what she used to entice the boys to sit through her class.

One day, my sister told me that the boys didn't want to come to Klump dinners anymore because they didn't want to have to "go to school" first. We delicately broke this news to GR; however, it didn't stop her from setting up dolls to teach or on occasion asking an adult to sit through her class. Needless to say, school and teaching made her happy.

I was never concerned with her ability to keep up with the workload. I think rest and recharging are extremely important. But I also believe productivity breeds more productivity, so staying busy can be a good thing. She's always enjoyed staying busy, especially since she spends so much time immobilized, doing medical treatments. It's a bit of a paradox for her "urgency in living."

She was also very hard on herself. She was driven and had high standards. She was that kid who, once she put her mind to something, was determined to figure it out. If nobody was going to show her or teach her, she would do it herself. In her afterschool program at the YMCA, she really wanted to learn hula hoop. Day after day, I would go to pick her up and find my four-and-a-half-year-old on the blacktop with a hula hoop. One day, I got there and saw that, sure enough, she had mastered it and was eager to show me all the tricks she could do while hula hooping. She was so proud of herself, and I loved her perseverance.

Ever since she learned to write, she'd wanted to learn cursive. I kept telling her that she'd learn to write cursive in second grade because that's when I had learned it. She didn't want to wait, so she took her "church money" (the money my mom offered her in exchange for attending church together) to buy books at the 99-cent store so she could practice tracing the letters.

When second grade started and the teacher told me they no longer taught cursive, I didn't know how to break the news to GR. It turns out she had already taught herself, and when the class was learning to put sentences together, she used her cursive to do so.

* * *

It was customary for me to start each school year with a note to the teacher asking for a meeting with them. This was recommended by her medical team. They gave me a small booklet that explained CF, the regimen, the symptoms, the challenges, and the fact that CF kids should not be penalized for missing school due to illness. I would explain to the teacher that each day typically presented some sort of health concern. GR may look completely healthy, but internally she was fighting daily. She loved school and never wanted to miss it; in fact, she would often go despite not feeling well, only to come home and crash.

I don't think many of the teachers paid much attention to my meeting or the booklet. That's not said to discredit them. I believe teachers go above and beyond more than most professionals. I just don't think they understood the gravity of CF; plus, they had so many other students and lessons to be concerned with. This meant that I was constantly having to explain why GR was either tardy or missing school altogether. In some cases, I pulled her out of school, for example, when she called me from the nurse's office to say that a student sitting next to her was coughing excessively. One day, I went to drop her off and upon greeting the teacher noted that she looked like she had the flu. She told me she was recovering from it but had to come in and teach.

"I hope you feel better," I said respectfully, "but Grace-Rose will not be staying at school today."

Most administrators understood – if they hadn't read the material I had provided, they at least allowed me to explain it. A few teachers would continue to punish her for tardies or absences. This led to complete distress. I believe she worked twice as hard as others to keep up. She wanted her work to be perfect, which was evident in its presentation. On top of extracurricular activities, she had three extra hours of medical protocols daily. Needless to say, it was frustrating.

I happened to meet an attorney at the school who specifically worked with kids with special needs. Her first son, who GR had befriended, was born with a learning and physical disability. When she asked if we had a 504 plan in place, I told her I didn't know what that was (though I did find it serendipitous that 504 is also the New Orleans area code.)

She explained it was a plan issued to the administration so they can't discriminate against a child for any disability. As long as GR's work was turned in and graded fairly, they couldn't punish her further.

My close friends were well aware of my concern with Grace-Rose being around sick people. It could easily land her in the hospital. Fortunately, they all had the courtesy to let me know if they or their children were sick so we could plan school and social engagements accordingly.

About halfway through second grade, some of these absences and tardies – as well as the heavier workload – were causing Grace-Rose to feel more discouraged with her grades. Even something as simple as a grade dropping from an A to a B+ would frustrate her. She believed she was taking longer to learn some of the subjects than her classmates. She also realized from celebrating class birthdays that she was always a year younger than the others. I discussed this with her teacher and we concluded that since she was the youngest and had health challenges, it might be wise to have her repeat second grade.

I was fairly comfortable with this decision. I had repeated ninth grade when I switched high schools, though it was my own decision and for a different reason. I also knew other parents who had made these decisions for their children. My biggest concern was for Grace-Rose's emotional well-being; she was already so hard on herself and I didn't want to make her feel as if something else was wrong with her. I also didn't want her to feel like we were making a decision based on her medical condition. I never wanted her to think that would impact anything she wanted to do. At the same time, just about every decision I had to make for the future was with a conscious awareness of what her declining health may look like.

It was a constant balancing act.

Once my decision was made, I spoke with the principal to see if repeating second grade was a possibility within the school and what the ramifications of that would look like. Again, her mental health was of particular concern. Third grade was when the kids broke into different lunch groups at different times, so it would be very noticeable that she was no longer with the older age group. We discussed moving her to another local public elementary school, which would require us to move into that district. The principal met with GR to assess her with the situation. He assured me that he thought she was mature enough and ready to handle it. The best plan would be to leave her in her current school, which we loved, because she was confident and he believed that she would adjust well.

GR and I spent many evenings at dinner, talking about what this transition would look like. I'd reassure her that it was the best decision for her age, her health, and her mind. I told her that while she was very smart, she was also very young. She was also aware of the fact that we could talk through any situation, concern, or decision together. I said, jokingly, "You do first grade once, you never want to do third grade three times, but sometimes you do second grade twice!"

Ultimately, it ended up being the right choice. She absolutely loved her second second-grade teacher. She loved all her teachers at this elementary school, but this one struck a particular chord. In fact, to this day she says once she's successful in her other career endeavors she wants to retire and teach second grade. It's pretty special when a teacher leaves such a strong impression.

However, there were some difficult aspects of the transition. As we had feared, when the lunch bell rang for the younger kids, which was earlier, I would see her holding her lunch bag in front of her face to hide the fact that she was with them. I wasn't sure what to do here, and I realized that perhaps some professional advice may be helpful. GR had a social worker in the hospital, but it wasn't someone she saw on a regular basis or who could help in this situation.

We went to interview a therapist. I firmly believe that interviewing is key to finding someone you can comfortably talk to and trust their advice. This therapist was a dream. She knew how to listen to Grace-Rose. She knew how to talk to Grace-Rose. She knew how to give her tools to help her get through this challenge. We were so grateful for her help, and devastated when she told us she was moving. Like the second-grade teacher, she made a profound impact, and I believe GR continues to use some of the tools she learned to this day.

The other challenge of repeating second grade was that the musical theater department had decided that only students grades three to five would be allowed to participate. This absolutely devastated GR. I had to beg the faculty to not let our decision to repeat second grade deprive her of one more thing. I pleaded with them to make an exception, since this rule was created after we made this decision. To do otherwise would have felt like a punishment.

Thankfully, they allowed her to participate – something we would appreciate even more as we came to realize how important musical theater was to her mental health.

That school was beneficial to GR in so many ways – so much of it was rooted in the attitude of the staff, starting with the principal's morning announcements. He would always end with, "Make it a great day or not, the choice is yours!"

Such a simple but poignant message.

Spicy Tuna on Crispy Rice

Recipe *adapted* from one of GR's favorite sushi orders, she especially loves the one at Kiwami by Katsu-ya in Studio City

Ingredients:

Crispy Rice:

- 1 cup sushi rice
- 1 cup water
- 1 tablespoon rice vinegar
- 1 tablespoon sugar
- ½ teaspoon salt
- Oil for frying (vegetable or canola)

Spicy Tuna:

- 6 oz sushi-grade tuna, diced
- 2 tablespoons mayonnaise (Kewpie mayo, if available)
- 1 tablespoon sriracha (adjust for spice level)
- 1 teaspoon soy sauce
- 1 teaspoon sesame oil

Instructions:

Step 1: Cook and Prepare Rice

1. Rinse the sushi rice under cold water until the water runs clear.
2. In a pot, combine 1 cup rice and 1 cup water. Bring to a boil, then cover and reduce the heat to low. Cook for 15-20 minutes until water is absorbed.

3. In a small bowl, mix rice vinegar, sugar, and salt until dissolved. Gently fold this mixture into the cooked rice. Let the rice cool.

Step 2: Form and Fry Rice Cakes

1. Once the rice has cooled, press it into a flat, even layer on a parchment-lined baking sheet (about 1/2 inch thick). Refrigerate for 30 minutes to firm up.

2. Cut the rice into small rectangles or squares.

3. In a skillet, heat about 1/4 inch of oil over medium heat. Fry the rice pieces until golden brown and crispy on both sides (about 2-3 minutes per side). Drain on paper towels.

Step 3: Make Spicy Tuna

1. In a bowl, combine diced tuna, mayonnaise, sriracha, soy sauce, and sesame oil. Stir until well combined.

Step 4: Assemble

1. Top each crispy rice square with a spoonful of spicy tuna.

2. Garnish with jalapeno, sliced avocado or green onions and sesame seeds, if desired.

* For a saltier, umami flavor top with Yuzu shio (yuzu salt)

TEN

MIDDLE SCHOOL – FIRST PANIC ATTACK

W here had the years gone? It seemed one minute GR was starting kindergarten and the next she was graduating from fifth grade and we were talking about where she would go to middle school. There was a lot riding on this decision; we were still considering the possibility of returning to New Orleans, but GR had also auditioned for a performing arts school in L.A. Her acceptance into their musical theater program basically sealed the deal. It was an amazing opportunity, and one she was very excited about.

This marked the end of those morning walks that helped us connect and mentally prepare for the day, and the beginning of a fun ritual we enjoyed on our drive to school. We discovered a radio show hosted by Ryan Seacrest called *Ryan's Roses.* Listeners would call in with the suspicion that their significant other was cheating on them or considering it. An on air staff member posing as a florist would then call the alleged cheater and offer them a dozen roses to be sent, free of charge, to anybody of their choosing. Sure enough, the accused cheater would often have the flowers sent to the "wrong person," resulting in the "truth" pouring out and an argument between the couple, moderated by Seacrest.

Ryan's Roses was a silly way to start the day and always resulted in a conversation about relationships. It also felt age-appropriate for GR, as it often opened up topics about the inevitable middle school drama she was facing. This transition period is one of the hardest for any kid. They are getting their first taste of independence while adjusting to the radical mental and physical changes of adolescence, and determining what true friendships and relationships look like in this process. Needless to say, there was never a shortage of topics of conversation at dinner, because there was a daily dose of drama to feast on.

GR typically used humor to process a situation. One night, she told me about her fellow students' obsession with vaping, then remarked that this was what all the "kids who thought they were cool" were doing. In order to mock this habit, she shared a photo of herself hiding in a bathroom stall at school with her midday inhaled antibiotic. The photo clearly depicted a prescribed medication; the caption stated, "This is how I vape!"

She absolutely loved this school, though it too didn't come without challenges. When you're in a highly competitive performing arts program, especially in a city like Los Angeles, the auditions and requirements are rigorous, to say the least. Along with the usual academic subjects, there were singing classes, dance classes, and acting classes. Each semester culminated in the performance of a musical, featuring two casts: the stage cast and the crew pit. They alternated roles each semester.

Grace-Rose's performances in *Hairspray, Shrek, The Addams Family,* and *Spamalot* are among my favorite memories from that time. During the summer, she would enlist in some sort of summer theater program for a creative outlet and to keep her momentum going. On stage or off, GR was always singing and dancing, even belting out show tunes while in the shower. It became a barometer for her mood. If I heard her singing, she was happy; if I didn't, I would be concerned.

GR loved watching theater almost as much as she loved performing. I vividly recall her very first Broadway show, *The Lion King,* when she was just three years old. It was after Hurricane Katrina, and we were visiting New York. I was still trying to decide if I was going to end up there or in Los Angeles. GR was on the edge of her seat the entire show, mesmerized. Since then, every trip to New York had to include at least one Broadway show. Between Broadway shows, The Pantages in L.A. and various London theaters, we've enjoyed so many shows together!

The Lion King, Wicked, School of Rock, Mean Girls, Beautiful, Tina Turner, Come From Away, Waitress, Hairspray, Funny Girl (with Beanie Feldstein) and Funny Girl (with Lea Michelle) Kinky Boots, Chicago, The Cher Show, Aladdin, Matilda, Mamma Mia, The Witches, Cabaret, Hamilton, Dear Evan Hanson, Beetlejuice, Moulin Rouge… I feel so fortunate to share these core memories with her.

* * *

However, this was definitely a shift for me. A lifelong athlete and sports enthusiast, I jokingly refer to theater intermission as "half-time." Back when I was studying fashion, Broadway was barely on my radar. My first job was in a sports store at Madison Square Garden and I took full advantage of all the free tickets offered to various sporting events.

I recall, while doing a trade show for the Rosie G clothing line at the Jacob Javits Center, trying desperately to get *Hamilton* tickets – and getting nowhere. Then, at the last minute, a friend of ours who knew someone in the show got us in – standing room only. We gladly accepted, and between GR's excitement and the incredible performances, I didn't even notice that I'd been on my feet for three and a half hours. I was thrilled with how our sales were going at the tradeshow, but this was certainly the highlight of the trip.

When we learned that Lea Michelle was starring in *Funny Girl* on Broadway, we knew we had to go. GR had been obsessed with Barbra Streisand ever since she first saw Lea sing Streisand's songs on *Glee*. In fact, she used Streisand's songs and monologues in her own auditions. I somehow managed to get tickets to opening night. The standing ovations were thunderous and constant, and by the curtain call, GR and

I both had tears streaming down our faces, recognizing what a long-awaited and full-circle moment this was.

After seeing *Tina - The Tina Turner Musical*, GR and I headed to Ellen's Stardust Diner, the iconic place where the waiters take turns belting out Broadway songs. There was often up to an hour wait, but if the show ended late enough and you got there right before they closed at midnight, you could usually slip right in for last call. Patrons were encouraged to sing along with the waiters, and GR always did. They were all incredibly talented, aspiring Broadway actors, and Grace-Rose would follow some of her favorites on Instagram. Whenever one of them made it to a cast on Broadway, we'd celebrate them.

She'd say, "I can see myself doing the same job when I come to college in New York."

It was drizzling when we left Ellen's Stardust that evening. Since we were only about twenty blocks from the hotel and not wanting to lose our excited energy, we chose to walk rather than hail a cab. And when the drizzle turned into a light but steady rain, she put Dua Lipa's "Don't Start Now" on her speakerphone to motivate us. We skipped the entire way back to the hotel as the rain picked up even more. It was pure magic.

I will always be grateful to GR for introducing me to musical theater and Broadway – and all the sentimental memories that came along with those experiences.

* * *

One summer, after a month-long visit in New Orleans, we were preparing to return to L.A. when Grace-Rose started feeling a little anxious. She had never enjoyed flying, but we did it often. She didn't want to miss out on anything. We had our pre-flight prep down: Dramamine, her playlist, and *Friends*, her favorite anti-anxiety show, to watch as a distraction. She would also find some sort of relic to carry that made her feel safer. This was before she had her pug, Buddy, who would become her support animal.

As we were preparing to board, we always checked people's carry-ons for the slight chance that someone else was carrying a vest (this medical equipment can't be checked in). If so, there would have been a concern about GR being in such close quarters with someone else with CF. We hadn't noticed anything.

Still, I could sense GR's heightened nerves as we stood in line to board the plane. Neither of us understood where this was coming from; again, we traveled frequently and had taken this particular trip many times before. Then, as soon as we started to walk down the aisle, Grace-Rose immediately turned around, her forty-pound vest in tow, and started running off the plane. I followed, apologizing to the others trying to make their way to their seats. I asked her what was wrong and became very concerned when she could not breathe to answer. I pulled out her inhaler, hoping that would help her get some air into her lungs. She had never experienced anything like this – could one of her lungs have collapsed?

A flight attendant called the paramedics, who came and started taking her vitals. Her heart was racing so fast, they thought she might be having a heart attack. I think it was because she had done her alb-uterol inhaler so many times that it sped up her heart rate. We mentioned Cystic Fibrosis to the paramedics, but they had no idea what that was. They offered to take her out on a stretcher to the nearest ER, but she didn't want to go. Trusting her instincts, I called my brother, who had dropped us off at the airport, and he turned back around to come get us.

We were in the car headed back to the house when it hit me: GR had just had a full-blown panic attack – her first. I rebooked our flights for a few days later, then we spoke with my brother-in-law, who had experience with panic attacks, about what had happened. To this day, we still don't know what caused it, though, thankfully, it turned out to be an isolated incident. We also don't know what triggered the anxiety and panic attacks that started appearing a couple of years later. How-ever, I can certainly imagine that being told your health is declining and that you don't have long to live—while also struggling to breathe—could be a major factor.

In fact, after that incident GR mentioned that she remembered hearing that she wasn't going to live past that age. That message must have manifested as a fear of getting on that plane – something she was already uncomfortable with.

Somewhere, subconsciously she thought if she got on that plane, she may not survive.

* * *

GR's former fifth-grade teacher had started a program where professional women would come and speak to the class about their careers. She knew Grace-Rose was a young business owner and invited her to participate. GR was so excited and honored. She thought it would be fun to tell students about her fundraising and clothing line, but what excited her the most was finally being able to teach a class. There was a Q&A session after each presentation, the students would flood GR with questions.

I was present for all these engagements, sitting off to the side, somewhat of an appendage as she needed no guide. But one time, a little girl in the back of the class raised her hand and said, "I have a question for your mom." I stood up so I could see her and give her my full attention. She then asked, "When you found out all of this about your daughter, how did it make *you* feel?" I was so relieved the bell rang at that very moment. The role of mother, father, caregiver, and friend often didn't allow me time to consider my own feelings, and now I wasn't sure I could keep it together long enough to respond.

I was reminded of the Brené Brown quote, "Vulnerability is not weakness, it's our greatest measure of courage."

Crawfish Monica-Style Street Tacos

A nod to the famous Crawfish Monica Pasta served at New Orleans Jazz Fest, combined with L.A.'s popular fish tacos

You can use shrimp too. Highly recommend the Louisiana crawfish as opposed to imported.

Sauce - 1 stick of butter, 1 pint of half and half, green onions, 2 tbsp minced garlic, creole seasoning (Tony Chachere's), and salt. Pink Himalayan salt works well.

Melt the butter in a skillet and sauté onions and garlic in it. Add salt. Add the crawfish and half-and-half and sauté until it bubbles. If using raw shrimp, slightly boil before adding to the sauce. If using crawfish, be sure to include the juice. Add creole seasoning, starting light as it has a kick, then taste and add as desired. Add panko or parmesan to thicken the sauce a little.

Buy small street tacos, cilantro, lime, cabbage and avocado.

I like to coat the shredded cabbage with the sauce, but you can add it separately or use coleslaw as well. Place all together in the taco, adding whatever amount of sliced avocado, lime, and cilantro you like.

You can also mix the crawfish into the rotini pasta (as they do at Jazz Fest) and add it to the taco with the pasta for extra carbs.

Tony Chachere's is a Louisiana creole seasoning. It's salty with a variety of spicy flavors and can be used on just about everything. The correct pronunciation is Tony "Sa-shury," but some of us like to call it Tony "Cha-chere's."

ELEVEN

ROSIE G CLOTHING – ADVOCACY

I had been designing clothes my whole life. I had known since I was a little girl that this was what I wanted to do. I went to Parsons Design School for summer camp after my sophomore year of high school, and this solidified my decision that New York City and fashion were my destiny. After attending Fashion Institute of Technology (FIT), I moved to Hong Kong to work for Fila Sportswear, then moved to Los Angeles, where the majority of local manufacturing was, to start my own line of contemporary clothing. I called it Pooch Clothing, after the affectionate nickname I had for my younger sister. I would end up having three clothing lines: Pooch Clothing, Saving Nola (after Hurricane Katrina), and Leah Milana. I had a store on Magazine Street in New Orleans and another on Ventura Blvd in Studio City, California. I sold my collections in these stores, as well as to various boutiques across the country.

It made sense that GR felt inspired to create her own designs, having watched me do it so many times before. Our tenth annual fashion show fundraiser, GR4CF #10, was approaching and would feature her first full collection. Included was a new design called the "two-panel dress." It had two separate one-shoulder panels that overlapped; one could be worn on top of the other or vice versa. There would be different colors and patterns that coordinated. The idea was that the kids could style themselves, just as GR always loved to do. At the end of the runway show, we decided to auction off the collection.

We didn't exactly have a plan for the line moving forward. However, when it was successfully auctioned off (thanks to my friend, Alexa, who outbid herself!), we came to the conclusion that perhaps more people would like to buy these clothes for their young daughters. We decided to create a new young girls' brand and call it "Rosie G" – the name of Grace-Rose's alter ego.

When she was very little, GR used to look at herself in the mirror while applying profuse amounts of lip gloss all over her lips particularly into the corners of her mouth. She would start talking differently to protect the lip gloss in the corners of her mouth. I also think it made her feel a new sense of confidence. She would talk and sing with this different personality. Witnessing the transition, my sister and I would joke that this must be her Cuban side coming out, and we called this other persona "Rosie G."

Whenever she started applying the lip gloss we'd say, "Oh no, here comes Rosie G!"

It was adorable.

Later, GR and I thought this would be a cute name for the brand; it also made sense because she might want to use Grace-Rose for something else. One of the first T-shirts we created was a baseball tee with the graphic "lost in lip gloss." This would kick off our first Indie Go-Go campaign to raise money to start the fashion brand. Thus, Rosie G, the clothing line was born.

I decided to put my full attention, money, and equity into building this brand because it was something creative we could do together. The wonderful story attached would further our advocacy efforts around CF. It quickly picked up momentum and we were able to use the brand in the fashion shows with young girls who absolutely loved modeling the clothes.

About a year later, our friends in Los Angeles convinced us to move the fundraising event there. Our factories were in Los Angeles, we were living in Los Angeles, and we had the potential to reach a bigger audience here. Plus, our friends pointed out, they would be available to help out and volunteer, as well as attend.

Our first Los Angeles GR4CF fashion fundraiser featuring Rosie G was held on the CBS Studios backlot. It was a picnic theme with food and ice cream trucks. We had a huge grass runway down the middle of the street with picnic blankets and baskets full of food. Converse was our shoe sponsor. We had a large silent auction. We decided to incorporate all of the youthful talent surrounding us into the event. We had young Disney and Nickelodeon stars, a nine-year-old DJ, and musical performances and dances from talented youth. Since GR loved dance, we held a dance audition at Millennium, a popular dance studio. We thought it would be fun to end the fashion show with a surprise flash mob as the runway finale. The event was such a great success that we couldn't wait to start planning the next one!

We started looking for sales reps and showrooms. I had fabric and blank t-shirt wholesale resources. However, we cut and sewed the majority of the tees ourselves because GR was so particular about the fabric and the fit. People always commented on how soft the tees were. She would come up with designs and wording to place on the tees and we worked with a graphic designer to help get them ready for print. We had a print warehouse that we worked with, as well as several manufacturers. We'd go downtown to the fabric showrooms and GR would pick a combination of sample fabrics for us to take to Roya, our sample and pattern maker. I met Roya when we first moved to L.A., and she helped me create custom designs. An incredible seamstress who adored GR, she was thrilled to assist us in developing these collections. GR was learning to design cohesive, vibrant, and marketable collections by thoughtfully selecting styles and fabrics, while also learning how to minimize material waste.

Once we had the season's samples developed, we'd arrange photoshoots at various locations based on the design theme or concept. GR would post castings on Instagram or invite friends to shoot the look books and the line sheets. She was also very comfortable speaking with adults and had no hesitation being in design or production meetings with me. She also enjoyed and was great at sales, showcasing her skills at trade shows, buyer's meetings and in-store events. We often spent weekends assembling collections, conducting fittings and photoshoots, and brainstorming themes and ideas for the next fundraiser.

The second event in L.A. was also on the CBS studios backlot and the theme we chose was "Carnival." It felt like a small circus, complete with a young Cirque Du Soleil troupe, Petite Cirque, performing throughout the event. At the conclusion of the runway finale, GR, after weeks of practice with one of the trapeze groups, slipped into a back room for a quick costume change. She then surprised everyone with a thrilling circus performance, adding an extra spark of excitement to the event.

The events were gaining traction and becoming incredibly popular amongst the youth via Instagram and other social media outlets. This was helpful for two main reasons: everyone was learning about Cystic Fibrosis and it was the exact market for the brand.

The following year, GR4CF #14 was held at the Houdini Estate in the Hollywood Hills off of Laurel Canyon. This theme, "Magic and Mystery," was one of our favorites. We had roaming magicians from The Magic Castle and a luxury car brand as one of the sponsors. We actually opened the show with a mini version of the car, driven up and down the runway by a four-year-old model – it was later auctioned off. The "backstage" where models dressed and had hair and makeup done, was in the main house and not attached to the area on the second-level garden where the fashion show was taking place. To disguise the outfits until the models got to the runway, we had them wear black magician capes and masks. Once the show started they would drop the cape, revealing their outfit, as they began to walk the runway.

Grace-Rose surprised the audience with her grand finale, walking down the runway in a blue silk chiffon gown. As the models made their final walk, known as the carousel, they each pulled a piece of chiffon from her waist as she spun around. The gown transformed into a mini dress, and as the models glided down the runway with the blue chiffon billowing, the song "River" by Bishop Briggs played.

Every detail of these fundraising events was meticulously planned. GR had a very specific vision, which was reflected in everything - from the themes and venues to the invitations, clothing designs, hair and makeup, shoes, food and beverages, and even the auction.

We'd spend an extensive amount of time with the music coordination. The DJ was very talented and able to spin great popular music throughout the evening, but the runway was GR's domain. We would measure the runway weeks beforehand and mark off the models' step count by taking turns walking the length back and forth for each model we had. She'd pick songs that she wanted to correspond with the styles and easily flow into one another. I loved witnessing her enthusiasm and excitement around the events, as well as her professionalism.

GR received several requests for interviews and was more than happy to comply. She appeared on the Hallmark Channel a few times, with friends in tow, to model new looks and promote the event and cause. She also had interviews on Good Day LA, KTLA, CBS, and Fox News - always poised and prepared, never fazed by the live set, cameras, or questions. It was truly impressive.

GR4CF #15 was held at the TOMS Corporate Headquarters in Marina Del Rey. We had been introduced to TOMS through our friend, Kate, who had worked in marketing at the beginning of the company and was friends with the founder, Blake. Kate had a very personal connection to CF. She was dating the actor Anton Yelchin, who had CF but was secretive about it so as not to disrupt his acting career. She wanted to get involved for this very reason. Kate told us that Anton was impressed with GR's "openness" about Cystic Fibrosis and inspired to do the same. It was incredibly sad and unfortunate that shortly after she told us this he was tragically killed in his driveway when his car malfunctioned. We had hoped GR and Anton would be able to meet (over the phone) as it wasn't safe to meet in person, and provide support and encouragement to each other.

* * *

Seeing how our brands were in alignment, TOMS was eager to support GR and the cause, and provide the models' shoes. We were always looking at different venues around town to see what might be a fit for the next themed event. TOMS and Rosie G had already established a relationship by doing some cross-promotional campaigns on social media and other outlets. The TOMS's Headquarters had a very open warehouse layout with a huge yard, a stage, an airstream trailer, and a winding slide connecting designers offices. It was fun and lent itself to our next theme, "Pop Art." This event had exciting entertainment provided by young musicians and dancers, as well as side activities throughout the spacious outdoor venue. Paul Mitchell, our HMU (hair and make-up) sponsor, did an amazing job with the models' makeup resembling Lichtenstein prints. Once again, there was a surprise finale – GR, carrying my eight-month-old niece Coco as she walked at the end of the runway show. They both wore outfits, designed by GR, to resemble Pop Art. Coco also wore a pair of TOMS from their brand new infant shoe collection.

The sixteenth GR4CF event, titled "Sweet Sixteen," featured a candy theme to celebrate both her upcoming sixteenth birthday and the year of the event. It was held at the SLS hotel in Beverly Hills. By this time we had an office in Burbank and our volunteer committee had grown exponentially. A good friend who worked in PR, was able to get Rachael Harris and Lauren German of the popular show *Lucifer*, to be our MCs. She even had the full cast attend the event, and secured a set visit for us to live auction as well. This was also the first event where we presented awards for Fashion and Philanthropy, Celebrity CF Advocacy, and a CF Medical Award. GR was maturing, and while we wanted to maintain a youthful vibe, we also aimed to elevate the experience.

Unfortunately, the COVID pandemic, which hit right afterward, significantly slowed down our fundraising efforts. However, the money raised from that event enabled us to start working on our mental health app for youth.

We had also been involved with CHLA's Make March Matter fundraising campaign. GR had attended their inaugural media kickoff day in 2015 as a patient and spokesperson, and continued to do so annually. During the month of March, several retailers, restaurants, and businesses across LA would participate. We would prepare for another large fashion fundraiser on behalf of the hospital that included events at the Americana at Brand and several Westfield malls.

We met with the Caruso team at the Grove and the Westfield team in Century City, where GR shared her visions for these events with the corporate teams, who then helped us work out the details. We had Rosie G kiosks in malls and pop-up shops, as well as marquee signs spread around the facilities. Both groups went above and beyond to make these events special, and the CHLA team was always present as well. It felt good to be giving back to the hospital that had given us so much.

One of our favorite Rosie G fundraising moments was when GR got a call from the producers of the Harry Connick Jr.'s daytime TV show in New York. They wanted to feature GR, then fourteen, as "The Super Kid." This wasn't the first time we had been approached by producers; in fact, GR had shot a pilot for a show about young entrepreneurs that did not get picked up. Now, the producers of *Harry* were offering to fly us to New York, pick us up from the airport, and put us up in the Hudson, a boutique hotel near the studio. Of course, we were one hundred percent in!

When we arrived, we went to see the musical *School of Rock* and the following morning headed straight to the studio. We had chosen local models we befriended via Instagram to wear the outfits featured on the show. The producers nervously ran through the segment and the script. GR was confident and excited. I mentioned to the producers that Harry Connick Sr. was our performer at her first GR4CF fashion fundraiser and I had a photo of him holding her while singing. I asked if during the commercial break I could share it with Harry, but they quickly let me know that he wouldn't have time as he would be preparing for the following segment. I brought the photo with me anyway and placed it under my seat in the audience, where the producers had me planted.

At the start of the segment, Harry asked GR where she was born and replied, "My heart just grew a little bit bigger" when he heard her say New Orleans, his hometown. He interviewed her a bit longer, followed by the fashion show, then GR was presented with a check made out to her foundation. When the segment was over, Harry said, "I want to meet Mom" and asked the producers to bring me to him. I proceeded to the taping floor and he pulled me aside to tell me two things: "First, you have a star here. Second, I lost my two young cousins to CF."

"Thank you so much," I replied, "and I'm so sorry about your cousins; your father told me. In fact, he was the performer at our first fashion fundraiser."

Tears welled up in Harry's eyes as he motioned for his daughter, Charlotte, to come see the picture of "Pawpaw" with baby GR. It was another incredible full-circle moment. After the show, we walked back to the hotel with the big fat cardboard check Harry had presented to GR. I have a photo of her walking down 57th Street, the wind so strong it pinned the check to her lengthwise, covering her entire body.

"Look, Ma, no hands!" she had exclaimed happily, but when we got back to the hotel, she admitted that she'd been in excruciating pain all day and couldn't wait to rest. I had sensed her discomfort at breakfast when she wasn't able to eat, but it was so typical for her to power through. No one would know from the way she carried herself, and she never complained, but eventually she would crash. I'm certain that the long flight, the altered treatment times, and excited energy of the city disrupted her schedule and routine. I also have no doubt that she thought it was completely worth it.

* * *

Rosie G clothing would end up being sold in Nordstrom, Bloomingdales, and several boutiques across the country. Grace-Rose had in-store events at Nordstrom in Colorado and Bloomingdales in Los Angeles. She would host events in New York during Fashion Week, as well as in her favorite New Orleans boutique, Pippen Lane. The hang tag on each article of clothing described the meaning behind the line and the designer, helping to spread more awareness of Cystic Fibrosis.

We'd built a beautiful community, but as Grace-Rose got older, her interests began to evolve into other avenues. I'll never forget these years that she was able to embrace the creativity and excitement of running an organization while making an impact.

Vegetarian Ramen

GR loves ramen, and it's loaded with salt and flavor. This recipe is *inspired* by our friend Jeff's New Orleans restaurant, Union Ramen. Jeff also helped us produce some of our first fashion and fundraising events as a partner with Renaissance Records.

Miso oyster mushroom ramen recipe:

Rich layers of umami with a miso-based broth, featuring oyster mushrooms for a savory depth and tender texture. Can also add several varieties of mushrooms.

Start by sautéing sliced mushrooms with garlic and ginger to enhance the flavor, then add vegetable broth (or a mushroom-infused broth for extra intensity), and bring it to a simmer.

Include miso paste, soy sauce, and a touch of mirin to add complex sweetness and saltiness to the broth.

Sometimes coconut milk is added for a creamy touch.

Once the broth is well-seasoned, add ramen noodles and cook until tender.

For garnish, consider including Bok choy, green onions, or soft-boiled eggs, which add color, freshness, and richness. Finish with sesame seeds or a chili oil crunch.

 * Add some Nori (seaweed) for extra salty flavor.

TWELVE

G-TUBE – FIGHT

As mentioned, I've always been athletic. Growing up without television meant more time outdoors, more activities, more after-school sports. We grew up playing tennis with my dad and grandmother, the coach. My dad was also very athletic, and we often watched him play tennis and basketball. My mom preferred racquetball and bike rides. Sundays were family days, which typically meant a bike ride to the JCC or tennis club for swimming or some athletic activity. I played basketball and volleyball and ran track in middle school; in high school, I switched to soccer and volleyball but would sometimes fill in on the tennis or track team if needed.

GR was not really interested in sports. While I introduced her to soccer, tennis, and basketball, it was clear that she preferred dance.

When she was four-and-a-half years old, she hadn't been feeling well for a while. I wanted to find some dance classes to help cheer her up and hopefully help increase her physical activity and energy. I happened to see an online flyer for a dance group called eKidz. It looked like a two-day dance workshop with famous choreographers at a school called Crossroads in Santa Monica. I thought it sounded like fun. I signed her up and when we arrived at the gym we discovered that it was actually an audition for a kids' dance team for the E-league. This was an entertainment basketball league for celebrities and industry members. It had been acquired from the NBA by a woman named Felisa. She had worked in the NBA and secured entertainment for many arenas, specifically in the dance community. Felisa's vision was to have a young dance squad perform at the games.

We were a little intimidated at first, as most kids were a bit older and had headshots, creative dance outfits, and tons of experience. As they were warming up and learning choreography, GR retreated to a quiet space in the back.

Seeing her discomfort and youth, Felisa walked over to speak to her. She encouraged her to jump into the audition and simply enjoy herself. Once GR got comfortable with the routines, she just started dancing and having fun. She was excited to return the following day. At the end of the weekend they announced the new entertainment dance squad. The eKidz would be composed of two groups, one of which was a new division of youth, GR's age. She made the squad and we instantly became friends with Felisa. Grace-Rose would learn routines and entertain during E-league games and public appearances in different locations, including L.A. Live, where the Lakers play. She found joy in dance and comfort on stage. The rehearsals would be held at well-known dance studios with popular choreographers around L.A., which is how we were introduced to the world of dance.

The Jr Lakers at the Hollywood YMCA allowed kids to start playing when they were five years old. As soon as she turned five I signed her up. She knew how much I enjoyed the sport and we both agreed it would be a fun activity to try. GR was the only girl on the team, which I assured her was totally acceptable. During one game, we were playing against Michael Rapaport's son's team. I vividly recall this because he is very passionate about hoops and so was his son. He also had a very loud cheering squad. GR didn't get the ball much, but in this particular game, with all the boys heavily guarded, the ball was passed to her.

Excited, she immediately started dribbling toward the net. It felt as though she was alone on the court and as if it was some sort of stage. She proceeded to shoot and score. The Rapaport side was cheering loudly, as our stands were being drowned out by our attempt to get her to turn around. She had scored for the other team!

I honestly don't know if it even bothered her because she was so elated by all the attention and the fact that she had actually made it in the basket. I once again recognized that sports may not be her thing, but the spotlight certainly was.

GR was an active and happy child. She was a good height and always on the skinny side but not in a way that looked unhealthy. However, whenever we went to the CF clinic, the doctors would find her BMI was less than twenty percent. They wanted her closer to fifty percent, so her weight remained a constant source of discussion and frustration. When she was seven years old, they added a new "appetite stimulant" drug to her multitude of medications. This one would increase her appetite but with its antihistamine properties, also cause drowsiness.

After a few months of taking it, I barely recognized my active, happy child. Although she was eating a bit more, she was practically a zombie. This wasn't a trade-off I was willing to make.

The way it was explained to me was that CF patients' inability to absorb nutrients, gain weight, and grow, has a direct effect on the body's ability to support the diaphragm. Since support of the diaphragm is crucial to supporting the lungs, without proper weight gain and growth, lung function would decrease more rapidly. I was intent on trying to get the required nutrients, calories, and fat into her. We were constantly reconfiguring the dosage of pancreatic enzymes that needed to be consumed before eating or drinking anything.

I understood that the G-tube worked for and helped many CF patients, but it also came with complications. Sometimes the tube would fall out, leaving a hole and exposure to the stomach. This could lead to an infection. It would also need to be replaced and properly washed and dressed from time to time. They said the main feed would take place throughout the night, meaning she would be constricted to one position of sleep while food was being admitted via a tube into her body. They told us she would wake up feeling as though she'd had a full Thanksgiving meal. I couldn't imagine how this would now affect the digestive system, knowing that even regular meals and snacks could be hard for her to process. Mornings were already arduous because we never knew how her tummy would feel.

What really concerned me was the fact that it would replace mealtimes and interrupt my favorite end to our day – family dinner. GR's biggest concern was that she would never be able to have a sleepover – not that those were really an option, though there were a handful of times I made special accommodations for her to do so. I would bring her to the party, sneak her out for treatment, and return her to the party to sleep. I would then pick her up first thing in the morning for treatment again. I could always tell when a parent was nervous if I left enzymes with them. I'd ask them to please remind her before she ate or drank anything, and though this sounded like a small request it could be uncomfortable to ask another parent to assume that responsibility.

She was pretty good at remembering, but I knew the distraction of playing with friends or the insecurity of having to take pills would sometimes be an issue. The only other sleepovers she had was each summer when we visited New Orleans. My sister, Aunt Pooch, and her then-boyfriend, now-husband would keep her for an evening. GR always looked forward to this because they would totally spoil her with movies, sushi, Pinkberry, and snuggles with their pug, Miles (this began her obsession with pugs.) I always appreciated this because it would give me an evening alone. I knew she was having fun and being well taken care of. There were very few people I could trust with her treatments and meds, and this gave me such peace of mind.

Another major concern with the tube was that it would finally make the disease "visible." Most of her dance outfits for performances and practices left her belly exposed or were very fitted. People would see the tube, leading to questions and body insecurity. I was so afraid she would begin to dislike dance, which had been such an incredible outlet for her both physically and mentally. The doctors, however, kept insisting on the tube. We even tried to come up with a cool design concept to cover it – perhaps an interesting, printed material that would serve as a "belly wrap" and make some sort of fashion statement.

BMI was so crucial that if there was even a half-pound weight gain we would go home and celebrate. I recall having cakes prepared for our return home and we'd put the amount of weight gain on the cake in celebration. Because what better way to celebrate weight gain than with a cake?! Ugh, constantly thinking about food, calories, and fat intake – with the goal of gaining weight – was so difficult for me. It's like trying to unlearn everything about healthy eating that you've ever been taught. I would sometimes feel the need to visit the gym twice a day!

It became clear that one of GR's dieticians did not care for me. She thought I was downplaying the need to place the tube. In fact, it was quite the opposite. It was a consistent topic of thought and decision-making for me. I sought outside opinions, desperately wanting a partner in this, if only to help me confirm how I was already feeling. My mother agreed that we had to consider the "mental health" aspect of the tube for GR. My father argued that the doctors knew what was best. Each trusted opinion just landed me right back in the middle. At the end of the day, it was up to me. I was the only one capable of making this decision for my child.

During one visit with this dietician, she asked GR what her favorite dinner was. Without hesitation GR, who was eight at the time, replied, "My mom's miso halibut over shredded cabbage."

The dietician glared at me and, without a word, exited the room. I wasn't sure what this would mean when the doctors returned to address it, but it was clear she believed I wasn't feeding GR properly by giving her wholesome, healthy meals. I felt the need to defend myself, to tell her that I added extra salt and butter to all of her meals, that miso paste is full of sodium, and GR was always given desserts.

I also fed GR pizza with extra cheese and burgers with bacon; I added the invisible powdered calories to just about everything. Yet, the dietician remained annoyed by the fact that GR loved sushi, either due to a sophisticated palette or the simple fact that it was easier on her digestive system. She also didn't like that we talked about shopping at farmer's markets, the Studio City one being a favorite.

What she didn't understand was that the market was about more than just food. It was a Sunday ritual for us, and one we thoroughly enjoyed. GR would swing on the swings and stop at all the fruit and veggie stands, sampling fresh peaches, cherries, or whatever was in season. She loved the Korean stand, her favorites being the tempeh, daikon, lotus root, burdock, and veggie or "healing broth." He would always explain the benefits of each, such as the daikon radish as a pro-biotic, burdock for the liver, and others for inflammation and natural antioxidants. She was impressed with this knowledge and took it very seriously for her health. When specific things were ailing her more than others we'd ask for suggestions from different vendors. From the "mushroom guy," she learned the benefits of cordyceps for lung health or lion's mane on brain health. If she didn't love the taste of something healthy for her, we'd find a way to hide it in a dish, like chocolate mousse made with cacao and avocado.

Sunday family dinners – or "Klump dinners," as we called them – were another precious tradition. We even went so far as to theme them so they were more interesting for the kids. We would choose a specific country or place and cook dishes from the region. Each person got to pick out something from that place to share at dinner. It could be anything from an outfit, a song, or a piece of art from a museum. It was a way for everyone to participate in the dinner conversation as well as learn something new.

Klump, our family nickname, had also become a verb around events and trips. It began on a family vacation to Vegas when GR and her two cousins were little. We were walking through the newly opened Wynn Casino when I mentioned that I needed to go to the bathroom. I would take GR with me, I said. My sister chimed in, "I need to go too"; then my mother said, "I might as well join you."

We all filed into the closest restroom, which had one stall. When we finally came out, my brother-in-law said, "You do realize that a few steps further is a large bathroom with multiple stalls. You guys always do everything together, you love to *Klump*!"

His words stuck, and soon we were asking each other, "Are we Klumping this weekend? Is this going to be a Klump vacation?"

We didn't have to ask whether Sunday Klump dinners were happening – they were a given and they wouldn't be the same for GR if she got the tube.

The dietician consulted with the nurse, and their conclusion was not in my favor. When she returned, along with the social worker, they rationally explained that I was compromising my daughter's health and future well-being by not placing the tube in her. It was time.

They sent me home with the prep paperwork and links to YouTube videos. Gunnar Esiason, now a young adult, shared his G-tube routine in the videos. It made me nauseous to watch them. When GR and I watched the videos together, she started crying - something she rarely did. This was the moment I made my decision clear.

Three months later, when we returned to our routine clinic, the team was surprised to learn that they would not be placing the tube in her. That was my final decision and, moving forward, I would prefer a different dietician.

I had taken a bold move; now I would have to prove myself. I had to do more to get that BMI up. I strongly believed it was the right decision for GR; I just prayed that her lungs didn't rapidly decline. If they did, I would never be able to forgive myself.

Miso Halibut with Shredded Cabbage

This is one of GR's favorite dishes and what got me in trouble with her dietician...

It can be almost any fish – halibut, seabass, kanpachi, salmon

I use a miso dressing or a miso paste that can be made into a sauce with broth or kewpie mayonnaise (easily found at H-Mart or in the Asian section of a market)

Cover the fish with the miso sauce of choice (I usually let it marinate first) and cook for whatever time the size and thickness of the fish requires. I like to sear both sides in a skillet first then place in the oven.

Shred green and purple cabbage and lay across a platter, place the cooked fish on top.

Use the leftover sauce to put back in the skillet with a little butter and a little broth. Cook until desired consistency of sauce and top over fish and cabbage, warming and slightly cooking the cabbage.

* Add a touch of Furikake seasoning salt on top.

THIRTEEN

GRACE-ROSE FOUNDATION – 501(C)(3)

W hen Grace-Rose was nine years old, we discovered an event called CF California Winemasters that was held on the backlot of War-ner Bros. Studios. The backlot would be filled with winemakers from all over California and Washington State. The fact that Warner Bros. was home to two of GR's favorite shows, *Friends* and *Gilmore Girls,* made it even more appealing.

At that time, CF California Winemasters had been founded twenty-eight years earlier by Barbara and Allen Balik, philanthropists and wine aficionados living in Napa. They had lost young friends to CF and wanted to help fund research. I was introduced to Barbara by a mutual friend who had suggested that my mom's new *Los Angeles Classic Desserts* cookbooks be gifted to the "Royalty table" during the event.

My mom had a successful commercial interior design firm in New Orleans, which was a major reason for the back and forth between Louisiana and California. She had also always loved cooking, so after Hurricane Katrina, when so many businesses were upended, she enrolled at Le Cordon Bleu in L.A. When the course was over, her good friend Kit suggested she write a cookbook. Kit had a series of classic New Orleans cookbooks, and her idea was that Mom could do one to represent L.A. Mom decided to focus on desserts, and I helped her procure the famous L.A. restaurants and chefs that were featured, including Wolfgang Puck at Hotel Bel Air and Spago; Chateau Marmont; Disneyland Café; The Polo Lounge at the Beverly Hills Hotel; La Brea Bakery; Porto's Bakery; Knott's Berry Farm; and many more.

The Royalty table at Winemasters consisted of regular significant donors and hosts of the event. My mother and I offered to bring selected desserts from Mom's cookbook to hand out to the table during the live auction. These would be accompanied by a signed copy of the cookbook as a special additional gift. The day of the event, my mother and I brought the desserts and cookbooks to a service area on the backlot. We were told to leave them for volunteers to deliver to the table at a specific time during the live auction. We happened to be watching the live auction, behind the scenes, when a special tour of a private vineyard in Italy came on the block. As the paddles went up, we noticed a gentleman at the Royalty table place the final bid of $53,000. My eyes began to tear up. I asked the volunteer in charge of delivering the desserts if I could take them instead. I wanted to personally thank this man.

I walked up the stairs to the elevated platform for the Royalty table, and as we placed the desserts and cookbooks in front of the guests, I turned to the man who had just donated $53,000 for one single item. I showed him a picture of GR and said, "Thank you, on behalf of me and my daughter, this is whose life you're saving." The man, whose name was Steve, gave me his information and asked that we please stay in touch. He had been introduced to this event by his close friend, Hal, another major donor. They were both avid wine collectors. Neither of them personally knew anyone with Cystic Fibrosis.

After this event, I was not only impressed but relieved to see how much money was being raised for this cause. Growing up, I had always been taught to write thank-you notes, and I had always insisted on them with GR after each event. We enjoyed going to the paper stores to choose stationery and accessories or stickers to decorate the notes and envelopes. I reached out directly to Barbara and asked if we could have the mailing addresses for their largest donors. We proceeded to send each one of them a handwritten thank-you note from Grace-Rose for their fundraising and support. They appreciated that someone with CF had noticed and acknowledged them.

Our relationship with Steve and his wife Emma grew as they invited us to dinners and events and introduced us to friends and other supporters. Steve, an attorney, offered to help GR establish her first 501(c) (3) and even become one of the organization's trusted advisors and committee members. With our own non-profit, we could raise money in any way we saw fit. We wouldn't have strict CFF guidelines to abide by. I completely understood the reason for the Foundation's rules and regulations, but I didn't want the creative aspect of our events to be compromised. I was afraid this would deter GR from her enthusiasm for fundraising and advocacy. The 501(c)(3) would also help us establish relationships in Los Angeles with bigger sponsors and donors. We would be able to donate directly to the Cystic Fibrosis Foundation, Children's Hospital LA, and the Make-a-Wish Foundation – all of which had made significant impacts on GR's life. We would later use the funds raised to create and donate coloring books to hospitals, as well as to start the development of our mental health app for youth.

* * *

When GR had started kindergarten, I stopped taking her to the gym with me nightly but I was still going on the weekends. I liked the facility, particularly because I was familiar with it. I enjoyed the classes, the basketball courts, youth activities, and the fact that it had built-in daycare.

One evening when I was upstairs lifting weights, I noticed a guy wearing a t-shirt that said "Fight CF." I was intrigued and had to ask if it stood for Cystic Fibrosis. He was surprised to hear that someone knew what CF was – a feeling I understood well, as GR and I were constantly educating people about it. We talked for a while and the guy, whose name was JR, shared that his niece, only a few years older than GR, had also been born with it. He immediately introduced me to his sister and niece's mother, via email, and I introduced him to Grace-Rose, who was at the gym with me. I contacted his sister, who lived in Toronto, and mentioned that I didn't have any other CF mom friends. We instantly bonded.

Shortly after, I changed my gym membership to one much closer to home. GR had outgrown the activities at the gym and was involved with other things. A few years later, we happened to be at an event for an organization we loved and supported – Children Mending Hearts, which raised money for arts and educational programs for underserved youth in L.A. We sold Rosie G clothing at some of their fundraising events, with proceeds going to CMH. As we got more involved with the organization, Grace-Rose would become their red carpet host and interviewer for celebrities in attendance. She would interview on behalf of the children's magazine *Mini-Maven*, which was one of the sponsors. At one event, where they were recognizing celebrities for their philanthropic achievements, they specifically mentioned Cystic Fibrosis. As I watched the cast of the popular show *Teen Wolf* get up to accept the award, I recognized JR, the guy from the gym. I had no idea that he was an actor on this show! He came over to our Rosie G booth after the award and introduced his whole cast to GR, telling them the story of how we met and the fact that she had CF, just like his niece.

After that, we became friends, with JR joining our committee and all of our fundraising efforts. He and Grace-Rose would bond over their love of theater and sushi. I was just grateful for his interest and support. He became very involved with our foundation and an avid promoter of the mental health app for youth that we were creating.

* * *

Our relationship with Winemasters resulted in Grace-Rose being invited the following year as a ten-year-old ambassador. She would help host the live auction and "Bid for the Cure" on stage with the father and advocate of a child with CF.

Grace-Rose was thrilled by the idea of being on stage in front of fifteen-hundred-plus people. Barbara, however, who didn't know her very well, was a bit apprehensive. We ended up meeting with the auctioneer a week before the event. This was when we found out that the father who had normally spoken on behalf of CF was no longer able to attend as his child was in the hospital. This made the director and the auctioneer both nervous, leaving such an important fundraising role in the hands of a ten-year-old!

I was not concerned at all; nevertheless, we met with DawnMarie, the auctioneer, at a coffee shop before the event. She and GR instantly bonded over their double names and, more importantly, their love of Barbra Streisand. I think this left DawnMarie at ease, witnessing GR's vivacious personality, projective voice, and maturity. At this point all they could do was have faith.

The night of the event when Grace-Rose was asked to come up for the live auction, she caught everyone's attention. This small child, adjusting the microphone, opened by saying, "Whether you live life looking at a glass half full or half empty, my glass runs over with gratitude for all of you here tonight."

The crowd erupted in applause. The message was clear, and this "Bid for the Cure" would raise the most money to date for that particular auction item.

Grace-Rose proceeded to thank each and every member who held up their paddle to bid. DawnMarie would share the microphone and GR would shout, "Thank YOU!" This became her signature declaration at every subsequent event as each paddle was raised for the "Bid for the Cure." The following year, Grace-Rose was asked to come back on her own as the new official ambassador for California Winemasters. She had asked if she could surprise DawnMarie before the "Bid for the Cure" by singing a Barbra Streisand favorite, "Don't Rain on My Parade." This meant we had to show up to the backlot extra early to meet with the sound technician and rehearse without spoiling the surprise.

When the time came and DawnMarie called her up to the stage, GR grabbed the mic and said, "I have a surprise for you!" Then the music started, and she belted out the song. DawnMarie was incredibly surprised and a bit emotional. The audience became even more motivated. The following year, she sang "Fight Song" by Rachel Platten, leaving the audience in tears. Each year the "Bid for the Cure" was rising!

The next year, as she was planning another performance and rehearsing, she noticed her voice had changed a bit; she wasn't hitting the notes properly. We realized that the new inhaled antibiotic she was taking for the recently diagnosed infection had changed her voice. It was raspier and made it hard to sing. She was devastated. Another joy this disease would take away, her voice. She was so insecure about it that she refused to sing at the event. When DawnMarie and Barbara asked what to expect this year, I explained the situation. Not wanting her to become too discouraged, they came up with a plan. Within a very small timeframe they managed to get their steadfast hosts, donors, and committee members to commit to singing lines from the Rachel Platten song, "Stand by You."

When Grace-Rose was called up to the stage, DawnMarie said, "This year, GR, we have a surprise for you!" The music started and, one by one, these hosts, donors, and committee members stood up singing lines of the song. Their faces were projected on the large screen for everyone to see. It felt so vulnerable and authentic. As they all belted out the chorus, "Know you're not alone because I'm gonna stand by you," GR began to weep. Happy, grateful tears that would encapsulate a moment never to be forgotten.

The presence and energy of fifteen hundred people standing by your side could undoubtedly symbolize one thing: healing.

The advocacy and fundraising on behalf of everyone involved with this event remains energetic. The "Bid for the Cure" continues to raise more and more money. Each year is a new opportunity for an onstage surprise.

As I was writing this chapter, I got a call from Olivia with CF Winemasters, letting me know that Barbara Balik, the founder and director, had passed away peacefully at home. We knew of Barbara's struggle with cancer, and at the past Winemasters event in May 2024 we learned it had metastasized to her brain. She was having some difficulty speaking, but against her family's advice insisted on being there. I recall seeing her on stage during the "Bid for the Cure" with Grace-Rose, and Dawn Marie exclaiming, "GR looks *and* feels freaking Amazing! And that's thanks to all of YOU!"

What a blessing for Barbara, after thirty-five years of hard work and fundraising, to be able to witness this moment, with her young ambassador, thriving.

In Grace-Rose's words, "Barbara, thank *YOU!*"

> I'd like to dedicate this chapter to Barbara Balik and her family for everything they've done for the CF community and the profound impact they've had on our lives.

Tres Leches Berry Trifle

This recipe is from Porto's Bakery, one of the oldest Cuban bakeries in L.A. It was featured in my mom's *Los Angeles Classic Desserts* cookbook, and one of the desserts we served to the Royalty table, along with a signed copy of the book, at Winemasters.

Ingredients -

Cake: Yield 12 servings (single serving small glass)
6 large eggs, separated
¼ cup granulated sugar, divided
¾ cup cake flour
3 tablespoons whole milk
¼ teaspoon vanilla
Preheat the oven to 350 degrees F.

Sift the cake flour and set it aside. Grease and flour either one 12-by-15-inch sheet pan or two 8-inch round cake pans lines with parchment or wax paper.

Prepare the cake batter by first separating the eggs, placing the yolks in one large mixing bowl and the whites in another.

Add ⅛ cup (2 tablespoons) of the sugar to the yolks and beat the mixture to the ribbon stage (reached when a spoon dipped into the mixture leaves a trail behind that is visible for a short while) about 3 to 5 minutes. The mixture should be pale yellow. Add and stir the sifted cake flour and milk into the yolk mixture in three stages. That is, add ¼ cup of the cake flour and 1 to 2 tablespoons of whole milk at a time, being careful not to deflate the mixture.

In the other mixing bowl with the egg whites, combine them with ⅛ cup (two tablespoons) of sugar. With an electric mixer, whip on medium speed to a soft-peak stage. The mixture will be shiny.

Add ⅓ of the egg whites and sugar to the yolk mixture and fold in the whites carefully so as not to deflate the mixture. Add the remaining ⅔ of the egg whites and sugar and carefully fold them in until everything is blended well. The mixture should be smooth and fluffy, not runny. Carefully spread the batter evenly into the prepared pan(s) and bake the cake for 8 to 10 minutes until light golden brown.

Milk/Cream filling for cake:

1 can (12 ounces) evaporated milk
1 can (12 ounces) sweetened condensed milk
¾ cup heavy cream

In medium-size bowl, mix the evaporated and condensed milks and cream until blended.

Remove the cake from the pan and flip it over by placing another piece of paper on top of it. Gently pierce the cake with a table fork every few inches and pour the milk-and-cream filling onto the cake, allowing the filling to penetrate the cake. Let this rest for 10-15 minutes to allow the cake to absorb the liquid.

Whipped Cream:

2 cups heavy whipping cream
1 tablespoon granulated sugar
¼ cup brandy or rum, optional
4 pints seasonal berries or fruits

In a medium, chilled metal bowl, whip the cream until soft peaks form. Add the sugar (and brandy or rum if desired) and continue whipping until no grittiness remains. In a glass dessert cup or drinking glasses, place a layer of the cake at the bottom, followed by a layer of whipped cream, place the berries on top of this and continue with another layer of cake, whipped cream and finished with fruit on top.

* To enhance the flavor, sprinkle a little Fleur de sel on top.

FOURTEEN

MUSICAL THEATER – SURGERY

Theater offers numerous benefits, including boosting self-confidence, enhancing communication skills, and strengthening self-expression. It encourages children to learn, play, and grow by stepping into the stories of others. Through role-playing, they can imagine life from different perspectives, fostering empathy and broadening their understanding of the world. Theater transports them to different times and places, encouraging shifts in mindset. It also cultivates camaraderie and teamwork, as performers learn to rely on one another. Additionally, it teaches valuable skills like time management and highlights the dedication required to memorize scripts, songs, and choreography.

I was amazed at how effortlessly GR memorized scripts and plays — not only her own lines but the entire production, including songs and choreography. This talent was something she definitely didn't inherit from me!

When GR was a baby, she had a crib painted by my sister Kate, sitting in the den of our childhood home. Positioned right next to the kitchen, it allowed Mom to keep an eye on her while cooking dinner whenever I had work to do. She would often turn on the soundtrack to *Chicago*, and as soon as the first few chords of "All that Jazz" started,

GR would grab the gate of the crib, hoist herself up, and rock back and forth in delight.

Since her first performance in pre-school of *Seussical the Musical*, she had been hooked. All through elementary she performed in musicals and attended a performing arts musical theater middle school. Drama, with its deep emotional aspects, was never her thing; she preferred the uplifting and musical aspect of theater. She needed this escape from "real life."

Freshman year of high school was the height of GR's anxiety. The challenges of her new school, coupled with the constant medical emergencies at home and medical teams surrounding us, only exacerbated her condition. It got to the point where she didn't want to leave my side for fear a panic attack or anxiety would creep in and suddenly take over.

When the drama program at school proved unfulfilling, we decided GR needed another theater outlet. A few of her former theater friends told us about a program they had participated in and we signed up immediately. GR would audition for *A Chorus Line*.

During her previous CF clinic and follow-up ENT visit, her doctor had recommended sinus surgery. Sinus surgery amongst CF patients is very common. Just as the breathing in the lungs gets constricted or infected, so do the sinuses, which are essentially the "lungs" in your head.

Once a CF patient undergoes their first sinus surgery it increases the need for additional surgeries. We were told, depending on the severity of the obstruction, it becomes as frequent as bi-annually or even monthly. We had been avoiding this and trying to manage her sinuses for years. Saline rinses, nasal sprays and even some essential oils. Unfortunately, it was harder to get medication into her nasal cavities in the way we could administer to her lungs. The polyps and nasal passage had become so obstructive that her breathing had become significantly more difficult, as well as her ability to smell or taste food. When you can't smell or taste food, your appetite decreases. That was something we couldn't afford.

As much as we wanted to avoid starting this new trajectory of indefinite surgeries, we both agreed it was time. The surgery would be scheduled two weeks before *A Chorus Line's* debut.

GR was absolutely thrilled when she got the part of Judy Turner, a character who plays a nervous and scatterbrained performer. This felt like just the right personality for GR to step into at this time. We then had to have a conversation with the theater directors regarding the surgery.

I privately pleaded with them to not let this interfere with her performance. Based on what we were told the recovery would look like, she'd only miss one rehearsal and then she could return with a nose bandage. She would only need to avoid heavy choreography or singing for a few days.

This was the first theater group she had participated in that was not aware of her pre-existing condition. All previous performances had been through schools, so of course they all knew. I had conversations with the teachers and administrators. We had a 504 plan in place so that her grades would not be affected by tardiness or absences. She was always skeptical of her roles in plays being diminished due to this. GR was afraid of not getting the role she deserved because the directors would be concerned that if she got sick or was hospitalized or had to miss a performance it would compromise the show. This was never the case. In fact, it was the opposite. Theater gave her something to look forward to and no matter how she felt she'd always persevere, even during tech week – which consisted of an entire week full of rehearsals before weeknight and weekend performances.

Tech weeks always secretly concerned me because of the long hours, late nights, and little time for food and additional calories, hydration, and medications. This, combined with late-night treatments, early-morning treatments, and homework meant less time for restorative sleep. I didn't express my concern to GR because I never wanted CF to get in the way of her life more than it already did. But I knew I'd have to monitor her much more closely. She would be exhausted after these shows, requiring extra time to recover and return to her routine.

A Chorus Line was giving her life and causing her anxiety to dissipate, so we were incredibly grateful when the directors, after being told about her CF and surgery, said they would allow her to keep her character and performance schedule.

The biggest fear of surgery for me was knowing that they had to anesthetize her. CF patients are considered high risk for anesthesia, particularly due to their potential for postoperative respiratory complications. Among all the patients and parents I followed in this community, nothing seemed more traumatic than surgery.

When they wheeled her away, she shouted out, "I love you, Mom! See you soon!" I remained stoic and calm, the traits I knew she appreciated in me. She was in good hands; all I could do was wait, keeping an eye on the clock. Approximately an hour and a half later, her doctor came out to tell me that the surgery had been completed and GR was in recovery. She then showed me photos taken of the interior of her sinuses.

She continued, "I'm sorry to have to tell you but when we were clearing up the polyps and frontal cavities we discovered that the infection was rampant."

This meant that the pseudomonas had grown and spread, and once GR had recovered they would have to go back in to surgically remove all of her sinuses. This would ultimately result in more frequent surgeries and more medications to treat the infection growing in her head. Looking at these photos, it was difficult to recognize her sinuses because they seemed to be blocked with a thick, dark mucus. I could only imagine how much she had been suffering. Then my guard came down, and I started to cry.

Before the surgery, a nurse had come in to explain the process and administer meds. He was tall and handsome, when he left, GR and I had a silly conversation about it. *Was he single?* We wondered, *Too young for me, too old for her?* Comic relief was easily our go-to.

I also had asked GR's permission to film her when she was waking up, and I'm so glad she agreed because it may be the funniest thing I have ever witnessed. In fact, whenever we need something to make us laugh, pulling up these videos does the trick. It was as though she had transformed into some version of an old southern woman. She had the drawl and the demeanor. The nurses couldn't stop laughing at her comments, she came out of surgery saying "I'm not lookin' too cute" and started calling me *guuurl* and asking me if I "went and got a Starbucks with that cutie nurse-a-mine" while she was in surgery. "Like, did ya'll go to the *clerb* and go dancin'?"

My response: "No, GR, I did not go on a Starbucks date while you were in surgery, and you were not in surgery long enough for us to go dancing at any club."

Making this interaction even more embarrassing-slash-hysterical was the fact that the nurse was on the other side of the curtain! GR's absurd commentary went on for about thirty more minutes until she was finally wheeled out of recovery. As soon as we got home she passed out. I didn't have it in me to tell her the outcome. That would have to wait.

I had noticed one of her coping mechanisms for dealing with the anxiety was taking noticeably deep breaths, particularly inhales. She would also nervously clear her throat. I'm not sure if anyone else noticed or if I was just hyperaware, but I wanted to help her alleviate it. What I do know is that this play and this group helped pull her back into herself and reminded me once again of the significant benefits of theater and creative outlets in general.

When it was time to audition for the next musical, *13: The Musical*, the director pulled her aside with concerns that the sensitive content about a teenager with MS may affect her. She assured them that no matter the content, this was exactly what she needed.

Thai Drunken Noodles or Pad Kee Mao

GR loves Thai food, drunken noodles being one of her favorites. Chicken is her first choice but it can be made with any protein such as shrimp, tofu or beef. You can also add more veggies for a Vegetarian version

Ingredients

For the sauce:

- 3 tablespoons soy sauce (or light soy sauce)
- 2 tablespoons oyster sauce
- 1 tablespoon dark soy sauce (for color and depth, but optional)
- 1 tablespoon fish sauce
- 1 tablespoon sugar (brown sugar works well here)
- 1 teaspoon chili paste or sriracha (adjust to taste)

For the noodles and stir-fry:

- 8 oz wide rice noodles (fresh is ideal, but dry noodles are fine – just soak or boil per package instructions)
- 2 tablespoons vegetable oil or other high-heat oil
- 4 cloves garlic, minced
- 1 or 2 Thai chilies, chopped (optional, or more if you like it spicy)
- 1 small onion, sliced
- 1 bell pepper (red or yellow), sliced
- 1 cup broccoli florets or Chinese broccoli, cut into bite-size pieces
- 1 small carrot, julienned or thinly sliced (optional)

- 1/2 cup fresh Thai basil leaves (or regular basil, but Thai basil is best)
- 1 cup protein of choice (chicken, shrimp, tofu, or beef – cut into bite-size pieces)

Instructions

1. Prepare the Sauce

   In a small bowl, whisk together soy sauce, oyster sauce, dark soy sauce (if using), fish sauce, sugar, and chili paste. Set aside.

2. Prepare the Noodles

   Cook or soak the rice noodles according to package instructions until they're just tender. Drain and set aside.

3. Stir-Fry Time
   1. Heat a large wok or skillet over high heat and add the vegetable oil.
   2. Add garlic and Thai chilies (if using). Stir-fry for about 30 seconds, or until fragrant.
   3. Add your choice of protein (chicken, shrimp, tofu, etc.) and stir-fry until it's nearly cooked through.
   4. Add the onions, bell pepper, broccoli, and carrots. Stir-fry for 2-3 minutes until vegetables are slightly tender but still crisp.

4. Add Noodles and Sauce
   1. Add the drained noodles to the pan, followed by the prepared sauce.
   2. Toss everything together to ensure the noodles are

coated well. Stir-fry for another 1-2 minutes until everything is evenly mixed and heated through.

5. Add Basil and Finish

1. Turn off the heat and add the fresh basil leaves. Toss until the basil is wilted slightly from the residual heat.

2. Taste and adjust seasoning as needed, adding extra fish sauce or chili paste if desired.

* Top with a little Thai Sea Salt

FIFTEEN

CHEESE-SURE – MOM'S INCIDENT

My family has always been obsessed with cheese. In fact, I think my mom may have possibly created the original charcuterie board. Each year during Mardi Gras, she would buy a wheel of stilton cheese and, on the night before Fat Tuesday, cut out the center and infuse a bottle of port wine into the cheese and let it sit overnight. Our house was close to the parade routes, which made it a convenient gathering spot. The port-filled stilton accompanied a large buffet awaiting family and friends who joined us.

We always had a large amount of this wheel leftover. We would have stilton grilled cheese sandwiches, stilton mac & cheese, stilton crumbled on salads and such throughout the year. Just as we had finished it, Mardi Gras would be rolling around again.

My brother-in-law's first visit to our home was during the holidays. Upon opening the refrigerator in search of a snack, he was astounded by not one, but two designated cheese drawers – one of which was overflowing and didn't quite close properly. At the same moment, my sister shouted out "I'm headed to the store, does anyone need anything?"

My mother promptly yelled from upstairs, "Don't forget to get more cheese!"

Well, you could imagine my brother-in-law's reaction. It's pretty much been a running joke in our family ever since.

* * *

On Saturday, October 28, 2017, I took Grace-Rose to a makeup artist's house in Beverly Hills. She wanted to use GR as a model to apply makeup and shoot images for her portfolio, and we thought it would be a great opportunity to get some new professional images as well.

That evening, we had been invited to a friend's annual Halloween party, which also happened to be in Beverly Hills. We lived on the other side of the hill, so this made plans for the day and evening convenient. Anyone who lives and drives in L.A. can relate. It was a long day, of which we spent the majority in the makeup chair and taking photos. When it was finally time to leave, GR said she was tired and her head was really hurting. She wanted to go home to do an extra treatment, rest, and take some medication; maybe then she would feel well enough to go to the party. We were both looking forward to going and, based on proximity, I really didn't want to have to drive back to Studio City only to come right back to this very same neighborhood. However, I needed to trust that GR was doing what was best for her health and body.

When we got home, she went to her room to do a treatment, lay down and take some medication. I returned to the kitchen to make a cheese plate. Cheese and fruit were staples I would typically serve as a grazing snack before dinner. I also didn't know how long we would be home before heading to the party and thought it would be a good idea to have something to eat before we left.

My mother had been recovering from a knee replacement surgery the month prior. She decided to have the surgery in Los Angeles rather than New Orleans because she believed I was the best person to assist her in recovery. After all, I was now considered a "caregiver" in my family. We had gotten accustomed to a physical therapist and a nurse visiting regularly to check in, do exercises, and help take Mom on walks. I also took her on walks, replaced and dressed the bandages, administered meds, and made sure she was using her knee recovery equipment. I also had to make sure she had enough food, specifically to accompany the pain medications she was taking that could make her dizzy and susceptible to falls.

This particular weekend, my father happened to be in town visiting. He and my sister had plans with Mom, which was why GR and I were able to spend the day and evening out. Mom had returned home and was resting before my sister planned to come back to pick her up for dinner. She was surprised to hear me and GR in the kitchen, since we weren't supposed to be home for several hours. Always one for a cheese plate and conversation, Mom joined and started asking how the makeup and photoshoot went.

She then began talking about the cheeses and how to make a cheese plate, which was a little odd as we'd been talking about the photoshoot. She began repeating the same thing over and over, and GR and I exchanged glances, giggling. My mom started to giggle too, though the situation felt a bit off.

I picked up the cheese plate and brought it to the dining area so we could sit and continue the conversation. GR chose to move into the adjacent open living area to lie down again, as her head was still bothering her. My mom asked GR a question, and I turned around to face her.

Suddenly, looking past me, she cried out in alarm, "Mom, quick, something's wrong with Mimi!"

As I whipped my head around I could see Mom trying to say something but not making any sense. She began stuttering, convulsing in the chair and foaming at the mouth. I jumped up and ran over to try to catch her so I could protect both her head and her knee from hitting the tile floor. Basically, I slid underneath her convulsing body to soften the landing as she fell out of the chair.

Grace-Rose grabbed my cell phone, called 911, and in a panic-stricken voice described what was happening to the operator. We had no idea what to do. The operator instructed me to put my finger in Mom's mouth to stop her from swallowing her tongue. I did this, but with her teeth clamping down so hard it felt as though I might lose my finger. The 911 operator stayed on the line with us until an ambulance and the fire department arrived.

I remember Grace-Rose, with Buddy in her arms, running all over the house looking for rosary beads or crosses, something my mom always had around. She started throwing them on top of Mom as we both lay on the ground, my finger still between her teeth. Mom had become somewhat frozen at this point and time seemed to stand still.

The fire department arrived first and Grace-Rose ran outside, Buddy still in her arms, to direct them into our unit. There were four men, moving the table and pulling off all the religious relics while asking questions about Mom's medications and exactly what may have brought this on. They then administered a shot to stabilize her, and by this time the ambulance had shown up. Grace-Rose also called my sister Allison, who fortunately was already on her way over to pick Mom up for dinner. She showed up just as the paramedics were moving Mom into the ambulance. I rode with her in the ambulance and Allison and GR followed.

As we sped to the hospital, I looked down at Mom and saw her face frozen in a state of anger and confusion. She was unresponsive but also looking at me as though she was crying for help. I just held her hand and kept talking to her, telling her that we were taking care of her and she needed to stay with us. When we reached the ER, she was rushed in, with a crash cart following.

Once she was stabilized, I waited with her until they had a hospital room. Our immediate family had been called and my father, as well as my brother-in-law Mark and their boys, arrived at the hospital.

Mark has always been one to use humor in the face of a stressful or dark situation. Actually, he pretty much always resorts to humor. We all gathered in her hospital room. Grace-Rose and I were trying to describe exactly what had happened and how it all started with a conversation around a cheese plate.

To this, Mark exclaimed, "Ohhh, she had a *cheese-sure*."

Everyone had a good laugh about that, including mom, who had no recall of what had happened or why she was in the hospital. Apparently, people don't remember having grand mal seizures because of the loss of awareness and memory during the seizure.

The following weeks, at the height of GR's anxiety and panic attacks, the house was filled with nurses, occupational therapists, physical therapists, cognitive therapists, and social workers. Every evening at dinner, Mom would ask, with zero recall, what had happened. She wanted us to explain the seizure over and over. I would excuse GR so she didn't have to relive the trauma, but I certainly was. When I explained this to one of the therapists who had been coming regularly, she had Mom write on a piece of paper, "I will not ask about the seizure, I will never remember it and it is triggering for both Leah and Grace-Rose."

When it inevitably came up again, I showed Mom the note and had her read it until it finally sunk in. We had notes plastered all over the walls, the front door and the bathroom mirror such as "Trust the Process" "Patience and Perseverance" and "Don't leave the house alone" – both reminders and affirmations.

She had memory tasks and cognitive skills coaching for the seizure, as well as in-home nurses and physical therapy since she was still recovering from the knee surgery. The house was a revolving door of medical specialists. Subsequently, there were more falls, including a few that landed us back in the emergency room with a subdural hematoma, sepsis, and an open wound cut on the forehead. It felt endless. I was unable to sleep at night for fear that there would be another fall or seizure. Every time I heard alarming noises in the middle of the night or throughout the day, my heart would start racing for fear of another incident.

Occasionally, when Grace-Rose witnessed a fall on her own, Mom would ask her not to tell me because she didn't want to worry me.

Of course, GR did, but the stress of the entire situation further exacerbated her anxiety.

Since I couldn't leave my mother unattended, I had to take her with me to drop GR off at school and pick her up. If she wasn't awake or ready, I'd leave her in one place with notes reminding her not to move. I was becoming overly anxious about everything; I remember my hands sometimes shaking on the steering wheel.

Grace-Rose's heightened anxiety and dislike of her new school made the days unbearable because she had no respite. School wasn't a safe place and neither was home. She needed me nearby at all times; she was afraid something might happen to Mimi. I too was afraid of this. For GR's mental health, I needed to keep them separate, but they both needed me close.

My days were consumed with administering meds to both my mother and my daughter, managing the medical staff who had taken over our home, setting doctors' appointments and therapy visits, and making sure meals were prepared. If we needed to go somewhere, like a CF clinic, I would have to find a friend to come and stay with Mom and have lunch with her. I even had a coffee barista who had become a friend to both of us, offer to come over for visits. It had to be someone Mom knew and it had to feel intentional. We'd tried hiring various caregivers to help us take breaks in the day or evening, but none were satisfactory to Mom.

I had no time to visit the factory and check on production and orders. After working so hard to secure the Nordstrom and Bloomingdale's accounts, I had to ask them, along with all of our other boutique clients, to allow us to relinquish this season due to a family emergency. Fortunately, everyone was very understanding, but this meant I couldn't fulfill these orders. I would take the loss on the collection, the samples, the photos, and the orders. It was my business, but I had no time for it.

It was during one hospital stay, when Mom got pneumonia, that we grew concerned that the family wouldn't be able to gather in Spain for our annual Klump Holiday vacation. She really wanted to take us to Barcelona.

We placed uplifting messages and photos in the hospital room. The largest one, directly across from her bed, was a photo of the Sagrada Familia, the famous Cathedral in Barcelona, which we would end up visiting that winter break. It's also known as "The Holy Family," which definitely felt appropriate.

Port-Infused Stilton

Murray's Cheese Shop on Bleecker St. in NYC has Stilton and Port samplings.   ·

Purchase a wheel of Stilton, cut out the center and place a bottle of port upside down in the center, allowing it to fully infuse the wheel, Serve with a baguette and sliced apple or pear.

Mom always said a cheese plate needed to *start* with four types of cheese:

Blue – Stilton

Creamy – D'affinois brie

Mild – Etorki or Essau Oraty

Colorful and sharp – Mimolette or Aged Gouda * extra salty

SIXTEEN

HIGH SCHOOL – BULLIES

Private schools in L.A. cost around forty thousand dollars a year. This was not an option for us. We weren't particularly excited about the public high school in our neighborhood and GR really wanted a school with a strong emphasis on theater and arts. The main option for this was a performing arts high school located southeast of Downtown L.A. It's extremely competitive and the audition process is nerve-wracking. Getting accepted would be a huge accomplishment; however, the commute to school would be grueling.

We had also heard of a small private Christian school that a few of our friends attended. I respected their opinion when it came to education and I was open to new prospects. It was on a beautiful hilltop overlooking mountains; in fact, some kids even rode horses to school. The campus was lovely and the classrooms were impeccably clean – something GR and I both quickly noticed, coming from public schools. I had always left Clorox wipes and cleaning supplies in previous school environments and the teachers were very appreciative.

This school clearly had a rigorous cleaning crew. The auditorium was beautiful and looked like a small Broadway theater. The playbills actually looked real, not like the parent/volunteer versions we were accustomed to. The teachers were sweet and considerate, particularly when we mentioned CF. The classroom sizes were small, about eighty kids per grade. GR was used to eight hundred at her middle school. What was *really* cool was that after freshman year she could declare a major to help prepare for college. She would then be able to build her course curriculum around it.

Everything about this school felt warm and cozy, and it wasn't quite as expensive as those other private schools. We could apply for financial aid. The only other parochial school nearby that we really liked was not an option. They had a student with CF and the space was too small, given the risk of cross-contamination of dangerous, invisible bacteria.

GR was still going to apply to the performing arts high school, but we needed a back-up in the event she didn't get in. There was also that insane commute to think about.

GR worked so hard on her audition, even practicing with acting coaches. When the day came, we got there extra early, not knowing exactly how long it may take or how many students would be at the audition. They were required to wear all black, fitted clothes with no logos and black shoes. Audition day was broken into parts, with students assigned alphabetically. GR was assigned to the first part, her last name starting with a B, and the large auditorium was full. The tension and nerves were palpable, not only from the students but the parents as well. Only one parent was allowed to accompany the student for crowd control purposes – at least that wasn't an issue for us!

The administration came in to explain the audition process and let us know where the parents could wait until it was over. The kids were broken into groups of four or five; they would wait with some senior students who would help them warm-up and prepare to be called in. Since GR chose to audition for their drama department, musical theater would be a separate audition once accepted. She had to choose two monologues – one comedic, the other dramatic.

GR chose the monologue "Bagels," from Barbara Streisand's *Funny Girl*, for her comedic monologue. GR has always preferred comedy and her timing is great. However, I think she has a lot to internally pull from for dramatic monologues, which is probably why she doesn't care for them as much. The dramatic one was from *Dirty Dancing*. She said the judges laughed at her comedic one and teared up at her dramatic monologue. This was a good sign.

The judges also asked them a personal question after their "slate," or introduction. If they were interested, they'd ask more questions of the student after. GR mentioned that they'd kept her for further questioning. Overall, I think she felt pretty confident. Once it was over, all we could do was wait. For two months.

We first got notification from the private school – she had been accepted, with a scholarship. This was a huge relief. But we both cried with excitement when we got the acceptance letter from the performing arts high school. GR was one of very few to be accepted.

This felt like a blessing and a curse. How would we decide?

We happened to be in Seattle for a buyer's meeting with Nordstrom on the date the decisions were due. When we arrived in the buyer's offices I excused myself to use the restroom. Upon my return, GR had already merchandised the entire grid and set out the line sheets and order forms for each buyer. I wasn't surprised. When the buyers entered, they were impressed and said, "Wow, you two work fast." I told them it was all GR.

This was our second time meeting with the team in Seattle and we were here to discuss the potential of a Nordstrom collaboration and possibly a private label. GR walked them through her new collection and we chatted about what all the kids were wearing – graphic tees, skater skirts, et cetera. We left with a sizable order in hand and decided to treat ourselves to a nice lunch and an exhibit at the Museum of Pop Culture. This was where we would make her high school decision.

We talked ad nauseam about the pros and cons of both, dissecting every detail. In the CF community this is referred to as "decision fatigue" – having to carefully overthink options, particularly when it comes to health considerations.

To get to the performing arts high school, most kids who lived in our area took the metro (which isn't as common in L.A. as in cities like New York), then a public bus, followed by a fifteen-minute walk.

The public transport concerned me for two reasons, GR's heightened anxiety, and the cleanliness, or lack thereof, that could lead to infection and further sickness. Going by car was pretty much out of the question. I don't particularly care for driving, and certainly not commutes that take about an hour and a half each way! This could mean up to six hours a day for me, driving to and from.

Public transportation would take about the same amount of time. This would require us to leave the house around 6:15 a.m., which meant waking up an extra hour and a half early to do treatments, eat breakfast, and get ready. I couldn't imagine a 5 a.m.-wake up for a full day of school, followed by theater rehearsals. If she returned home anytime between 6 and 8 p.m. she'd still have to do treatment, dinner, homework and get ready for bed. We had heard about how long these days were for kids who went there, but they loved theater so much that it was worth it. What they didn't have to consider was an extra two or more hours a day of treatments and the potential decline in health. Lack of sleep and exhaustion would only exacerbate GR's condition. This didn't even take into account tech and rehearsal weeks.

Another concern of mine was that CF would be a problem for the administration. I had discovered that the older GR got, the less accommodating the teachers had become. I'm not exactly sure why, but perhaps they thought she "looked healthy" and was using this as an excuse to miss school or be tardy. Some teachers even made snarky comments to her about it, and when she came home distraught, I'd call an immediate meeting with the teacher and the administration and educate them once again about Cystic Fibrosis. It went something like this:

"CF is an invisible disease that attacks all of your internal organs. It is life-threatening, with no cure; the average life expectancy is currently in the early twenties. GR has to do *two to three hours* of medical treatments EVERY single day; she takes forty pills or more per day and has frequent hospital visits. And she is a child on the 'healthy end of the CF spectrum.' She doesn't even know if she'll be able to attend college, and she's working harder than anyone just to maintain some sense of normalcy and get through high school. This is why she has a 504 plan, and this is why I'd appreciate it if you would respect it."

Of course, GR never wanted me to make a fuss about it or cause her to stand out any more than she already felt she did. However, if it meant a teacher was going to drop her hard-earned A to a B simply because she was tardy, she agreed with my tactic.

I was afraid that the performing arts high school would not choose her for larger roles due to her CF. I had seen this happen before. This was in addition to my larger fear that her health would decline due to the long hours, the lack of sleep, proper nutrition, and the long, anxiety-ridden and unclean commute.

We talked about moving closer to the school, but this would mean leaving the comfortable condominium we had finally found in the neighborhood we loved. I wasn't familiar with the neighborhood near the school, nor did we particularly like it. All our friends were nearby.

We considered the fact that there was an opportunity to finally go to a private school. She had always been curious about wearing a uniform, something that excited her (though, to be honest, I think that was largely due to the fact that she was into *Gossip Girl* at the time!)

The administration seemed to genuinely care about her condition, and the fact that she was such an advocate and young philanthropist. It seemed as though she'd get a great education in a nurturing, clean environment with a stellar theater department. The commute was also a comfortable drive against L.A. traffic. We felt we had made the decision, though I was still slightly conflicted and I know she was too. No matter how much we talked about it, I truly couldn't think of a better choice.

This would be the first time we made a decision primarily based on Cystic Fibrosis. I never wanted that to be the case, but with GR's declining PFTs (Pulmonary Function Tests) and all the information I was being fed from the CF community via the Foundation or social media, it felt inevitable. I remember one CF mom asking me where GR wanted to go to college and when I told her New York City, she quickly responded with "Oh, so you plan to move with her, right?" I told her that was in fact my plan. This woman had lost her daughter right after college and believed letting her go away was a contributing factor. That school had been in the same state; I couldn't imagine letting GR move across the country and having to manage all of her healthcare needs without me.

While GR will always regret not going to the performing arts high school, I still believe it would have compromised her physical health.

The first private school orientation was a week before school. GR was anxious but excited when I dropped her off. When I picked her up, I immediately noticed that she didn't have the same energy. I asked her how it went and she just replied, "I can already tell…these aren't my people."

We remained optimistic. School started and she began to make friends, which took more effort than usual because she was the "new girl." The majority of these kids had been in this small school together since kindergarten, and by the time GR entered in ninth grade they had long since established their friend groups. She did connect with a few of the girls; however, two boys in particular made it their mission to bully her and make her feel unwanted.

It started with obnoxious comments like, "Why are you even here?" and "I don't like your face," then they started running into her in the cafeteria and knocking over her lunch tray. I seriously could not believe kids were still doing this AND getting away with it. They would kick her school bag, push her in the hallways, make mean comments as they passed her seat in class. And on. And on.

GR certainly wasn't shy and knew how to stand up for herself, confronting them head-on and telling them to leave her alone. She did everything she could think of to try to mitigate or ignore the situation. She tried to avoid them, she asked teachers if she could switch classrooms so she would not have to hear their rude comments or be harassed by them all day. This would prove to be more difficult due to the small class sizes. For whatever reason, these boys were determined to make her feel unsafe, unwanted, and miserable. As much as we understood that their behavior stemmed from their own insecurities, it was still no excuse for such treatment.

Our homelife at the time was also extremely difficult with Mom's medical situation. It felt like a hospital, with medical equipment everywhere and rotating teams of physicians throughout the day. School was meant to be a respite from it all, but it was just the opposite. I believe GR felt as though the walls were closing in on her, and her anxiety and panic attacks were becoming much more frequent. I know it felt like this to me and I hadn't even experienced this level of anxiety before.

Once GR felt as though she had exhausted every option of dealing with these boys on her own, she decided to go to the school counselor. She was very apprehensive because she had always seen shows where the counselor only exacerbated the situation. I went with her and asked the counselor to arrange a meeting with the boys' parents. She replied that it was against school policy but assured us she would handle the situation. I couldn't help but wonder, where does bullying fit into your school policy? When GR asked how she planned to address it, the counselor said she would give the boys a warning.

"Please," GR said, "do not mention my name."

Apparently, many other girls had issues with these kids as well. They told GR to just accept it because there was nothing they could do. As far as we were concerned, this was not an option. It needed to end and the boys needed to be properly disciplined.

Two days later, I got a call from the nurse's office, with GR frantically and breathlessly saying, "Mom, I can't breathe. I think my lung collapsed. Please come get me."

I found out that the counselor had in fact mentioned GR was the one reporting them and this made them so angry that they decided to stand up on the lunch tables and shout out to everyone that

Grace-Rose had called them out to the counselor. She raced to the nurse's office in a panic. When I addressed the counselor about her intention and GR's very specific request not to mention her name, she just apologized. She then suggested that in order to avoid these kids she could join others in a designated room during lunch to watch movies. I was shocked that rather than disciplining these kids for their abhorrent acts they were asking my daughter to hide! That was it. I was done. I told them we would not be returning. School could wait; GR was smart and would catch up. Her mental health had to be my top priority now.

I would have to postpone the Nordstrom order. I couldn't spend the amount of time on the factory floor, in quality control and managing production that was necessary to get the order properly delivered. We couldn't afford to make mistakes with these early shipments as they would determine the growth of the business. I spoke to the buyers and asked that they allow us to pass on this collection's order and graciously give us another opportunity the following season. They did. This also meant that the samples, line sheets, fabric orders, photos and everything used to create, market and sell the collection would not be useful. That season would have to pass.

I started researching methods to help. Therapy, acupuncture, salt rooms – I was open to anything. We discovered a new meditation center that had just opened up in our neighborhood called The Den. It was offering a fixed-price monthly unlimited membership. I thought it would be an opportunity to try several different forms of meditations, including those to relieve anxiety and help sleep patterns, as well as hypnosis, sound baths, reiki, relaxation and more.

Friends would take turns having lunch or dinner with my mom if a nurse wasn't available. She still couldn't be left unattended. We went to one or two meditations a day. I remember the women in the classes, some of whom were neighborhood friends, looking perplexed to see a fifteen-year-old there in the middle of the day. I wasn't sure how GR would acclimate to any of it but she was finding different techniques that worked. She also had a few favorite teachers that she found relatable and we'd book around their schedule. This meditation center was comforting and grounding. We had also interviewed four different therapists until we found one that GR felt comfortable with. She was specifically trained to help adolescent girls with life-threatening conditions or disabilities. After a month designated to these practices, it seemed as though GR had been somewhat restored. We would continue to use them, but the time had come to figure out other school options.

She decided to prepare to re-audition for the performing arts high school. In hindsight, I don't think she stood a chance; people didn't decline this acceptance the first time, it would be unusual to be given a second opportunity. I had written to the administration explaining the unusual circumstances and to please consider giving her another chance; however, it was ignored. This time was more nerve-wracking than the last. Everything stood on it.

We also had to consider how she would finish freshman year and have a realistic backup plan for sophomore year. She had several friends who were actors and familiar with online and homeschool programs. We gathered recommendations and found a suitable one that she could start right away. She would work with an online school counselor to finish the course work she'd started. She'd also have to hustle to catch up on what she had missed, including taking courses throughout the summer.

We had heard of another large public school in nearby Burbank that was known as the "Glee school" because the hit TV show had been modeled after their glee club. They also had a strong performing arts program. It was in a different district from ours, which meant I would have to get office space in Burbank. This worked out because we could use the space to hold committee meetings for the Foundation and fittings for samples and fashion shows. As part of our due diligence in enrolling we had to check with the administration and school nurse to see if there were any other kids with CF at the school.

When we met the school nurse, she told us she had worked in a hospital with kids with CF and was very familiar with it and how strict their separation needed to be. This reassured us. She then told us that they had two other CF students at the school but it was pretty large, roughly 3,500 students.

She wasn't able to give us any more information, other than the fact that one would be a senior with different interests than GR. We believed this meant perhaps sports but not performing arts. The other was an incoming freshman. She claimed that with the school being so big and the kids being in different grades they would likely never cross paths. Since she couldn't reveal who these kids were, we asked if she could give the parents my email and number in the event they wanted to contact me – and give the students GR's name and Instagram so they would know who to avoid. This wasn't just about HIPAA confidentiality – as important as that is – but a potentially life or death situation. It's the one rare condition that all involved need to know about.

I never heard from the parents and GR never heard from the students. Perhaps they never got our information. Now we had another obstacle to consider: high school amongst two other CF'ers. GR was struggling with the fact that she'd constantly be looking over her shoulder, avoiding anyone who looked sick or coughed, and constantly be wiping down surfaces in such a large institution. High school was certainly not working in our favor.

We called her social worker at the hospital and asked if she knew these kids – a possibility since there were only a few L.A. hospitals with a CF care center for youth. We simply wanted to know that if they were patients at CHLA and, if so, did either of them have b-cepacia, the more lethal bacteria. She did, in fact, tell us that she had one patient who was a senior at that high school, as the nurse mentioned. She couldn't tell us any more but assured us that she didn't think it posed a threat. She did not know the other kid.

Now my concern was that GR's anxiety, which we had been working so hard to manage, would return given the possibility of being in proximity to other contagious kids. The best comparison to this would be the early days of the covid pandemic, when you had no idea who was sick and could potentially infect you.

GR, being a very social kid and not wanting to be stuck at home any longer, decided to give it a shot. At the beginning of school she reunited with two other friends who had left the same private school. This was refreshing. A few weeks into classes, after a missed test due to the CF clinic, she ended up in a makeup test room with other students. These students were a combination of freshmen and sophomores. She brought her Clorox wipes and proceeded to clean her desk. A few minutes into the test she heard a boy coughing. It sounded like a wet CF cough; she was acutely aware of the difference. She quietly went up to the teacher and asked if she knew if there was a freshman boy in the room who may have CF. When the teacher replied, "Yes," GR asked to be removed from the room. The teacher stuck her in a supply closet to finish the test.

When she told me after school, I immediately went to the nurse to make her aware of our concern that they would constantly be in the same room making up work due to doctor's visits or illness. This needed to be addressed.

Shortly thereafter, GR overheard a kid in Spanish class making fun of his cousin's trouble breathing and coughing.

"He just got out of the hospital," he said, "He's really sick, like he's gonna die soon."

Startled, GR turned around and asked who he was talking about. He told her his sick cousin was in ninth grade and he had some disease called "cys…" He couldn't pronounce it. "You mean Cystic Fibrosis?" GR asked.

"Yeah, that's it."

GR replied, "I have it too."

Visibly uncomfortable, the kid awkwardly said, "Oh, well I have diabetes."

With an eye roll, she asked if his cousin had an Instagram account.

When he told her, she discovered that it was the same boy she had suspected in the makeup test room. At least she could now identify him and keep her distance. After school she told me this story and we looked at his Instagram together. He did not look well at all, and there were several photos of him in the hospital. She sent him a thoughtful DM letting him know she could relate and who she was so he could avoid her too.

A few weeks passed with no incidents; if GR had any make-up work she found a math teacher who allowed her to use the classroom separately from the other students. Then, in early October a job fair came to the auditorium. Freshmen and sophomores were required to go at the same time. As GR was perusing the tables in the crowded auditorium, she felt someone bump into her. When she turned around and recognized the kid with CF, she ran into the nurse's office and called me with panic in her tone. This kid wasn't well, she could have contracted a lethal bacteria, she couldn't manage this anxiety anymore. She would have never known if she hadn't discovered on her own who he was. She could have had several more run-ins; the school couldn't ensure her safety. I picked her up immediately and asked the administration, nurse, and counselor for a meeting the following day.

When I returned the next morning to meet with the staff, I explained what had occurred on more than one occasion. GR had figured out who one person at the school with CF was, but there was another student and running into him or her could literally be a matter of life or death. The nurse began to cry. Having had experience with CF patients, she understood the severity. I asked the vice-principal if he had any suggestions for GR finishing school at home. This was not our first choice, nor was it ideal for GR, but it felt like our last resort. He mentioned their Independent Learning Academy (ILA) specifically created by the school for young actors. We had heard of it; in fact, GR had a friend in this program. They'd have access to all school amenities and be able to graduate with the class but take lessons at home, or on set. They would be required to meet with a teacher/advisor once a week at a separate location and could schedule test times there as well. This sounded like our best option.

At this point, the school counselor chimed in. "There are currently no spots left and there is a waitlist."

I looked her in the eye and said respectfully, "I'll be expecting your call this afternoon to let me know you've found a spot for her."

The principal, nurse and counselor all shook their heads in agreement, understanding the extremity of the situation and the fact that I wasn't taking no for an answer. That afternoon I got the call that GR had been enrolled.

As we grew accustomed to ILA, we had to consider the silver linings. Travel wouldn't be an issue, she could attend trade shows in New York, do school work at the beach, visit family in New Orleans, schedule buyers trips, and even host a New York Fashion Week event. She could work from anywhere and create her own schedule. She'd always been extremely disciplined, so this didn't concern me at all.

The other silver lining was yet to come: when Covid sent everyone into isolation, she was already accustomed to it. Plus, it meant more time with Buddy, her emotional support pug and best friend, who left her side only for mealtimes.

The first week of March 2020, a reporter called to interview GR for a story about the concern with this new coronavirus, especially for those with pre-existing pulmonary conditions. She agreed to the interview and photoshoot, not quite sure how serious this was. However, she noted, "It's kind of like the whole world has CF now." The next week, as we were issued a lockdown, a large photo of her surfaced in the *L.A. Times* as the face of Covid.

Bolognese

One of GR's favorite pasta dishes. This pappardelle version is *adapted* from Sylvain restaurant in New Orleans, owned by our friend Robert LeBlanc. He was also instrumental in helping us with our first fashion fundraisers at his newly opened venues and continues to support GR4CF.

Ingredients

- 1 lb. ground beef (or a mix of ground beef and pork)
- 1 tbsp olive oil
- 1 onion, finely chopped
- 2 cloves garlic, minced
- 1 carrot, finely chopped
- 1 celery stalk, finely chopped
- 1 can (14 oz) crushed tomatoes (or tomato sauce)
- 1/4 cup tomato paste
- 1/2 cup beef broth (optional, for extra richness)
- Salt and pepper to taste
- Fresh basil or parsley, chopped (for garnish)
- Grated Parmesan cheese (for topping)

Instructions

Step 1: Sauté the Vegetables

1. Heat Olive Oil: In a large skillet or saucepan, heat the olive oil over medium heat.

2. Cook the Vegetables: Add the chopped onion, garlic, carrot, and celery. Sauté for 5-7 minutes, until softened and fragrant.

Step 2: Brown the Meat

1. Add Ground Meat: Add the ground beef (or beef and pork mix) to the skillet, breaking it up with a spoon. Cook until browned and no longer pink, about 5-6 minutes.

2. Season with salt and pepper to taste.

Step 3: Add Tomatoes and Simmer

1. Add Tomatoes and Tomato Paste: Pour in the crushed tomatoes and add the tomato paste. Stir to combine.

2. Add Broth: Can also add some heavy cream for a creamier sauce or a red wine for a richer complexity in the sauce. Stir well.

3. Simmer: Reduce heat to low, cover, and let the sauce simmer for 20-30 minutes, stirring occasionally, until thickened and flavors are well blended.

4. Serve over Pappardelle pasta or pasta of choice

* Sprinkle a little Hawaiian Red Sea Salt on top.

SEVENTEEN

MAKE A WISH – BIG DREAMS

In April 2017, GR was asked by her social worker at CHLA if she'd like to be considered for a "special wish" from the Make-A-Wish Foundation. This amazing charity was inspired in 1980 by a seven-year-old Phoenix boy, Christopher James Greicius. Like most kids, Christopher had an idea of what he wanted to be when he grew up – a police officer – but he was losing his battle with leukemia. A friend of the family came together with his fellow law enforcement officers to "deputize" Christopher and make him a cop for a day. They even gave him a uniform. Christopher died a few days later, and his mother, who saw the joy getting the wish had brought him, started Make-A-Wish. Since then, it has grown into a huge organization, granting wishes to children with life-threatening conditions all over the world. Some kids lived for years afterward to talk about how special it was. For others, it was the last time they would do something outside of the hospital. Either way, it was an incredible gift, shedding light on dark times.

GR and I gladly accepted this introduction. When they reached out to send volunteers to our house for an interview, we got excited. After chatting with them for a couple of hours, they agreed GR would be a perfect candidate. "Dream up your biggest dream," they told her, "and let us know what that is and we'll work on accelerating it." They also said that

167

wishes could sometimes take a year or more to be granted due to exist-ing "wish kids" agendas and scheduling. They also couldn't involve a cash exchange, like paying for bills or education. It had to be an "experience."

GR started dreaming, and we had a lot of fun thinking of different ideas. Then, in August, while we were in New York for a tradeshow, she came up with a really big dream. It was almost a lightbulb moment. Whenever we had successful market weeks, sales events, or trade shows we liked to celebrate our success with a little treat. Many times, it would be dinner at Nobu Malibu overlooking the ocean or some sort of sushi treat. This time, our treat would be seeing Hamilton on Broadway, for which I had miraculously scored tickets.

When Peggy, the little sister of the Schuyler family, entered the stage, GR turned to me and said, "Do you think they'd let me be Peggy for a show? I could totally learn those lines and that choreography!" The role was less prominent than the main characters.

Wow, I had no idea, but it certainly felt like a big enough dream. When we had our follow-up meeting with Make-A-Wish, GR shared her very ambitious idea. This was easily the biggest show on Broadway and definitely the most difficult to get tickets to. Its significance was monumental.

A few months later, they told us that despite their best efforts, for bureaucratic reasons they were unable to grant this wish.

We completely understood and started thinking of other ideas. We had to think quickly as time was running out on the age limit for wish kids. Finally, we came up with the idea of having GR doing a red-carpet interview with a popular celebrity news network at a big movie pre-miere. GR always enjoyed being on TV but was typically the one being interviewed. She thought it would be fun to flip the script. She could ask the questions and attend a premiere. Make-A-Wish got to work, and in May 2019 they granted her wish! A few days before the premiere they asked us to meet them at The Beverly Center, a large, upscale mall nestled between Beverly Hills and West Hollywood.

When we arrived on the third floor, there were volunteers holding large mylar balloons that read Grace-Rose, Wish Kid. They had gifts for her and took her on a shopping spree to find the perfect outfit for her red-carpet debut. She tried on dresses, shoes, handbags and jewelry until she found the perfect "look." We then got milkshakes and discussed the day-of plans. A limousine would be sent to the house to pick us up; we would be staying at the Loews in Hollywood across from the famous El Capitan theater and treated to mani/pedis and a sushi dinner. We picked Kathy Sushi, from her childhood, as it was nearby on Franklin Ave. The following morning the limo would pick us up, take us to E-News on the Universal Studios lot. She would be sent into hair and make-up and given a script of the show. Various correspondents would come in to talk to her throughout the process, and host Jason Kennedy would make sure she was ready for the segment, which would be taped and aired the following day. The limo would return to pick us up, with cameras in tow, to get her to the red carpet to prep for the premiere.

Typically, both parents are invited to join; in our case, we invited my mom. We all watched the premiere of *Aladdin* together, then Mom and I were sent to a VIP press box while GR was sent to the carpet. She would be hosting the interviews with Erin Lim, an E-News correspondent, who was a sweetheart. They had spent a few hours bonding on the carpet before the film and had a natural chemistry. There was a dizzying number of cameras, interviewers, and press.

They allowed me to stand behind her, out of sight, to watch.

Once the interviews got under way, GR stood by Erin's side and was introduced to the celebrities as a Wish Kid. She was then given the opportunity to interview them. She had taken notes and prepared questions. Erin was so impressed that she allowed GR to take some of the interviews over completely. She spoke to Oscar-winner Helen Mirren and Candace Cameron Bure, as well as the stars of *Aladdin*. After she interviewed Will Smith, he asked if her mom was nearby. He wanted to meet me. The camera crew grabbed me and introduced us. He said, "You've done an amazing job, Mom, you've also raised a star!"

I thanked him and looked at GR, overcome with pride and gratitude. Once the interviews were complete, we were all invited to the VIP afterparty at The Roosevelt hotel nearby on Hollywood Blvd. We ate, danced, and mingled with celebrities. My mom had a blast. Of all the stars in the room that night I couldn't help but think that my little one shined the brightest.

It aired the following night, with a segment of GR starting out on E-news, being shuffled to the red carpet and conducting interviews. We all had fun reliving the moment. After that, GR became an advocate for the Make-A-Wish Foundation, appearing on news shows to speak about it and hosting red carpet interviews for their galas. She was also invited to co-host their National Convention in Phoenix. Not fully understanding everything it would involve, we agreed.

On October 23, 2019, they flew us to Phoenix for the convention. When we got to the hotel we noticed the large script for the event waiting for us, but GR only glanced at it. We couldn't imagine this large script was only for her! We spent the evening in the hotel with room service and movies, resting up for her packed schedule. The following day, she would attend a walk-through of the event and have about thirty minutes to rehearse in the auditorium prior to hair and makeup. It also happened to be my forty-fifth birthday, which provided an unusually fun way to celebrate!

When she got to the hair and makeup chair, GR meticulously studied the script as she realized the magnitude of her role. It was also her first time using a teleprompter. Her co-host, another Wish Kid, was quite shy. I was a little bit shocked that they had their National Make-A-Wish Convention – a four-hour evening culminating with a dinner party and fifteen hundred attendees – resting in their hands. GR managed to pull it off remarkably, once again, filling me with awe and pride.

What made it even more memorable was the fact that we were able to spend the rest of my birthday weekend in Sedona – a treat that we both felt we needed and deserved.

Honey Pie Pizza

GR loves this pizza from Follia in the Gramercy neighborhood of NYC. Obviously, NYC has a huge array of pizza options. This restaurant happened to be close to her first dorm.

Easiest ways to make:

Buy pizza dough, roll out and top with tomato sauce, mozzarella, hot soppressata and basil. Drizzle honey on top. (Or purchase a pepperoni pizza and drizzle hot honey on top)

* Add a dash of Maldon Garlic Sea Salt (for a little more flavor)

In the way of honey... and small apps

They also make delicious crostini with ricotta, mascarpone and burrata cheeses

Typically topped with extra virgin olive oil but we like to drizzle honey, or hot honey

Easiest way to make: Slice baguette, add a little olive oil and bake until toasty.

Spread the cheese of choice, drizzle oil (for savory), honey (for sweet), or hot honey (for sweet & spicy). Top with pimento

* Add a dash of Maldon Chilli Sea Salt (for additional kick.)

EIGHTEEN

TRIKAFTA – MIRACLE DRUG

Dum Spiro, Spero
(Latin phrase meaning, "While I breathe, I hope.")

To anyone questioning science or the life-saving potential of pharmaceuticals, I suggest reading Bijal P. Trivedi's *Breath From Salt: A Deadly Genetic Disease, A New Era in Science, and the Patients and Families Who Changed Medicine Forever.*

As the book begins...

Cystic fibrosis was once a mysterious disease that killed infants and children.

In 1974, Joey O'Donnell was born with strange symptoms. His insatiable appetite, incessant vomiting, and a relentless cough—which shook his tiny, fragile body and made it difficult to draw breath—confounded doctors and caused his parents agonizing, sleepless nights. After six sickly months, his salty skin provided the critical clue: he was one of thousands of Americans with cystic fibrosis, an inherited lung disorder that would most likely kill him before his first birthday.

The gene and mutation responsible for CF were found in 1989—discoveries that promised to lead to a cure for kids like Joey. But treatments unexpectedly failed and CF was deemed incurable. It was only after the Cystic Fibrosis Foundation, a grassroots organization founded by parents, formed an unprecedented partnership with a fledgling biotech company that transformative leaps in drug development were harnessed to produce groundbreaking new treatments: pills that could fix the crippled protein at the root of this deadly disease. [1*]

Before the discovery of Cystic Fibrosis, it was said that if the mother kissed her baby's forehead and it tasted salty, the baby wouldn't live very long.

When I first went to the Volunteer Leadership Conference in Washington DC, I was completely overwhelmed. I recall learning about drugs in the pipeline and the evolution of such. It would take years. I would remind myself over and over, "If I can just keep GR healthy enough for the next fifteen years, this very promising drug may become available."

I had followed Lea Farroane and Tiff Rich, aka the "Salty Cysters," and Gunnar Esiason on Instagram and listened to their podcasts. I followed several other people in the CF Community on social media, as this was our only real way to "connect". It was helpful to hear parents' perspectives and concerns, as well as medicines and techniques that worked for them. I took GR's medical care by her CF team very seriously; however, I was also open to adding Eastern or Holistic approaches to her regimen as well. I would always discuss it with her team beforehand so as not to conflict with any of her current medications. I followed some of the young CF adults to try to understand what independence might look like and if it was even possible. I was

---

[1*] Trivedi, Bijal P. (2020) *Breath from Salt: A Deadly Genetic Disease, a New Era in Science, and the Patients and Families Who Changed Medicine Forever.* BenBella Books.

inspired by their openness and refusal to give up. It was, of course, also very difficult to follow them when they regressed in health – or worse, needed a lung transplant, something very common with CF as lung function declines and is the last option.

In 2018, the promising, long-awaited drug Trikafta (its name a combination of three medicines) began clinical trials. Speaking openly about it, Gunnar and Lea had both entered the trial after experiencing a decrease in energy and lung function, as well as an overall health decline. They both had big dreams and still held on to a promising future. They had supportive and loving families and friends, and they were strong pillars in the fight against CF as advocates and fundraisers.

When a clinical trial is administered, no one knows who gets the actual drug and who gets the placebo. Immediately, Gunnar was excitedly sharing his increased energy levels, ability to run miles again and overall better health. Lea's health continued to decline. She had to be listed for a lung transplant.

In December 2018, I was in a meeting when someone mentioned a social media reference. As I opened my phone to check Instagram, Lea's page unexpectedly popped up. She had passed away while awaiting transplant. I excused myself to go to the bathroom, as I was too emotional at that moment. If only she had received the actual drug, one we'd all been waiting decades for, she might still be with us.

As I learned more about the research and drugs in the pipeline, and further read in Trivedi's book...this was one of the parts that gave a sense of hope.

By mid- 2017 Vertex had several trials in progress, the hypothesis was that if children began treatments almost from birth, patients might be spared both untimely death from early lung damage and the later horrors of CF that children who survived infancy faced. If one of the triple combos worked, CF would no longer be much of a pediatric disease.

On July 18, 2017, Fred Van Goor (head of CF research for Vertex Pharmaceuticals) had just sat down for dinner on a family cruise when he got a call from David Altshuler, Vertex's chief scientific officer, in Boston. He instructed him to sign an NDA and call him right back. Atlshuler had just seen the results of the phase II trials for the two new correctors - VX-440 and VX-152 - in the triple drug combos. After the first few numbers, Van Goor pretty much stopped hearing what Altshuler was saying, awestruck by what he'd heard so far. The results that Altshuler was sharing were exactly as Van Goor had expected. But actually hearing how the patients' lungs responded to this new medicine, how dramatically it opened them up, made the news real and overwhelming. He leaned on the ship's railing and wept, as other passengers gave him a wide berth. Van Goor was unprepared for the pent-up emotions that had been swirling in him for the last eighteen years, and for how desperately he wanted these treatments to work. [2]

* * *

In November 2019, GR became eligible for and received her first dose of Trikafta. Within a week she was feeling changes. I watched her awkwardly, daily, waiting for indications that it was working. I immediately noticed that her persistent cough, especially at night, had dissipated. It was something I had always listened for. Her stomach pains, regularly in the mornings but many times throughout the entire day, became less of a complaint. She was breathing better - more through her nose than her mouth. She continued to take all of her other medications and do her daily breathing treatments because it wouldn't be determined until the next phase of the trial what, if anything, could be eliminated.

Everything she had been doing, for years, had been preventative. This drug was actually changing her body on a cellular level. We remained in a state of hopeful concern, waiting for some huge reaction or side effect, which we still wouldn't know for a while.

She had been taking Trikafta for a month when it came time for our Klump holiday trip to Santiago, Chile in December. My mother liked to plan and help orchestrate trips to destinations she found interesting,

---

[2]* Trivedi, Bijal P. (2020) *Breath from Salt: A Deadly Genetic Disease, a New Era in Science, and the Patients and Families Who Changed Medicine Forever.* BenBella Books.

beautiful, historic and may not necessarily be on the top of everyone's list. These trips would be carefully planned and full of activities and meals. GR and I would often miss out on some of the events because of treatments, long travel times, or her not feeling well.

In some instances, we'd have to search all over a foreign country for a nebulizer that had blown out or an adapter that could satisfy the elevated hertz on her vest. However, none of this would stop us from participating. This trip, we noticed a much smoother transition than usual. When she missed a treatment due to the long flights we would typically notice it in her health right away. This trip, the whole family could tell the difference. She was also gaining weight!

By the time she was due for her January clinic checkup, she had gained several pounds. This was perhaps the most outwardly visible distinction that the drug was working. It was so unusual that she became concerned. Her clothes were no longer fitting and she didn't like her new, fuller face. Indeed, the nurses excitedly announced that she had gained eight pounds! In the past, this was an impossible feat that could take two years, not two months. Her PFTs had already increased to the high 90s, something we hadn't seen since middle school! I was holding back tears; I think we all were.

The dietician then asked GR how it felt to finally be able to gain weight. GR told her that she didn't like it because she could no longer wear the clothes she really liked, her face was filling out in a way she didn't recognize, and she didn't feel comfortable in her skin. The dietician mentioned that she'd have to drastically change her diet and begin counting calories. I never believed in counting calories, but rather simply noticing them. My theory was as long as you ate healthy and exercised you could determine what your body was responding to and what worked for you. Calorie-counting seemed like it could become very consuming and make you overthink what should be the natural process of eating. I understood the dietician's logic; I just didn't want it to now create some sort of an eating disorder. We knew her CF diet was never "normal" and figured that if this drug was working so well we could eliminate all the snacks between meals.

No more extra salty chips, extra cheese or sauce or butter. We could stop the late-night ice cream, cookies, and high-calorie shakes. Some of these habits were harder to kick because of how used to them she had become. And quite honestly, who doesn't want to be told that late-night break-and-bakes are actually good for you!

GR did start counting calories because now she'd have to go from the required 5,000 calories per day to an average person's diet of 1,500. She maintained her dance classes, but also started taking some yoga classes and a gym routine of different levels of acceleration and incline on the treadmill.

Of all the CF parents I followed on social media, there were two moms in particular I had really connected with – they also had children the same age as GR and with similar journeys. We became friends and would typically check in on one another a few times throughout the year to see how our kids were doing and how we were holding up. One of these moms I had grown especially close to because we had several things in common and both of our children wanted to attend college in New York. We chatted about the fact that we'd follow them, and it felt comforting to know that she recognized the need for that. I'm certain that when I mentioned that I'd be "going to college" with GR, people judged me. This was one parent who could completely relate and validate my concern. Our kids had also started Trikafta at the same time. We kept saying, "When is the other shoe going to drop?" We had been so programmed to believe that if your child ever felt relatively healthy, don't get too comfortable.

In February 2020, a few months after GR had started taking Trikafta, we were invited to visit Vertex Pharmaceuticals – the company who had created it – in Boston. My father, who was living there at the time, joined us at the large, brand-new building on Boston's waterfront. Vertex had outgrown their original home in Cambridge.

When we arrived, a lab technician greeted us and gave us lab coats and goggles. We were asked to leave our phones behind as nothing could be photographed or recorded. The tour followed the process of creating the drug: research, development, testing, more testing, packaging, and so on. I was fascinated by the process, the number of scientists involved and the money required for one drug from start to finish. What was even more fascinating was the amount of time it took. There were large signs at the entrance and exit of the building reading "ALL in for CF." We certainly felt grateful.

The impact of Trifkafta really hit home when GR returned to her ENT. This was a doctor we really liked and who had performed two of her sinus surgeries. We were prepared for this to become a routine surgery. When we went to this follow-up visit, I had finally grown accustomed to watching her put a lightbulb and a camera stick into her nose and throughout her sinuses. GR would sometimes comment "I think you might be poking my brain!" I still don't know how she could tolerate this, especially without the numbing spray that would typically accompany the procedure. GR didn't like it because it would slide down the back of her throat and that feeling was far more uncomfortable.

This time, as the doctor and I watched the monitor that was connected to the camera on the scope in her nose, we were both astonished at how clear her sinuses looked. I thought, if this is any indication of what her lungs may now look like, this drug is miraculous. It made me incredibly emotional.

It's important to mention that although Trikafta has drastically changed the lives of so many people with CF, it is still not a cure. It is a very heavy medication required twice daily, along with some of the other CF drugs. It is incredibly expensive and it only affects people with common (and some rare) CF mutations of which there are literally thousands. This means not all patients are candidates for this drug.

* * *

Another prominent person in the CF Community, also mentioned in Trivedi's book, is Robert Coughlin, a former Massachusetts state congressman who was now serving as president and CEO of the nonprofit Massachusetts Biotechnology Council (MassBio) in Cambridge. Like Joe O'Donnell, he had been working for years to help Vertex reach their goals - and for a very personal reason. His son Bobby, at the time of Trikafta drug trials, was fifteen and sick with CF-related end-stage liver disease. His son had one copy of the F508del mutation, and one copy of a second, rare mutation. (Just like Grace-Rose) In 2017, Bobby was too sick to participate in the phase II clinical trials. Coughlin tried not to follow this particular trial too closely for fear that it may not help his son's rare mutation. However, on July 18, 2018, Vertex CEO Jeffrey Leiden called to tell him that the triple combo was working for patients like his son. When Coughlin told his family at dinner that evening there was a palpable sense of relief and joy. They were keenly aware of how quickly Cystic Fibrosis could hurtle forward, progressing to a point of no return. Coughlin's children had seen their young cousins and other family members die from it.

He was grateful that Bobby was one of ninety percent of CF patients who would benefit, but he couldn't stop thinking about the last ten percent. He knew how awful that felt. Vertex had overcome a big hurdle, but they weren't at the finish line. [3]

Another important sidenote is that some CF patients who started taking Trikafta reported experiencing severe depression and suicidal thoughts, leading them to stop taking it. I find it so ironic that this "life-saving" drug also had a potentially life-threatening side effect. I am also fascinated by the effects of substances in different people's brains. GR, fortunately, did not experience that.

Again, while it has indeed been a miracle drug for us, it is not a cure. We will continue our awareness and fundraising efforts until CF is eradicated.

This chapter is dedicated to Joe O'Donnell, for his extraordinary commitment to CF, his venture philanthropy, and his outstanding efforts in fundraising. He has left behind a true legacy.

---

[3] Trivedi, Bijal P. (2020) *Breath from Salt: A Deadly Genetic Disease, a New Era in Science, and the Patients and Families Who Changed Medicine Forever.* BenBella Books.

Southern Mixed Greens

GR loved my large pot of greens and it was a great way to add more fiber to her diet.

Collard Greens
Mustard Greens
Swiss Chard
Flat leaf kale
Spinach
Shredded cabbage

In a large pot – start with butter and a little olive oil and salt

Add chopped onions, garlic and leeks – cook down

Add a little stock (we love the veggie "healing broth" from the Korean stand at the Studio City Farmers Market, but you can use beef, chicken, or bone broth as well.)

Start adding chopped greens, introducing the thicker greens first (i.e. collard, mustard & kale.)

As these cook down, add more butter and salt; add vinegar and sugar as well.

Add the softer greens (i.e. chard, spinach, cabbage.)

Keep stirring on low heat as they all cook down... season to taste.

* For a slightly saltier taste, add soy, ponzu and fish sauce.

NINETEEN

COVID – FACTORY SHUTDOWN

In February 2020, my good friend's event company was hired to produce the premiere of a movie and asked me to work the event. Kristin Banta Events (KBE) had always volunteered to help with our fundraising events and, knowing my experience, often hired me as a freelancer on hers. This one was a no-brainer because it was taking place in New Orleans. Kristin, who is based in L.A., had worked in NOLA before; in fact, the previous year, she had been hired by the actor Darren Criss and his fiancée, Mia, to plan and produce their wedding in New Orleans. Knowing GR would be traveling with me and trusting her professionalism, Kristin asked if she wanted to work these events as well. When Grace-Rose found out the wedding was for a former *Glee* cast member, she enthusiastically agreed. She practically "Gleek'ed out" when the after-party transformed into a full concert, with former cast members taking the stage to perform.

This film premiere happened to be during Mardi Gras season, so we decided to stay. This was another benefit of her being homeschooled.

Mignonne, now Dr. Mary, has been one of my dear friends since kindergarten. Her family owns a Mardi Gras crew and ball, and I had grown up attending all the balls with her family. Then, when we were in high school, Mignonne became queen of the ball and I was asked to be on her court. I had entertained GR with stories about this, she also knew Mignonne's daughter Lynn, who was the same age and would become queen the following year.

When Mignonne found out we were in town she invited us to attend. GR had so many questions for me afterward, and it was interesting to hear about it from a new perspective. Something that was so familiar to me but so foreign to GR! It made for a fun and educational conversation.

After this trip we headed to New York City to meet with the Bloomingdale's buying team and host our first New York Fashion Week event. We had collaborated with a cashmere sweater brand named Lingua Franca, which focuses on causes and giving back. We would be hosting a Q&A about Cystic Fibrosis and mental health initiatives and a party at their new Madison Avenue flagship store. Our friend and Grace Rose Foundation supporter, JR Bourne, was in town and agreed to co-host the Q&A.

One month later we would go on lockdown.

GR, who was all too familiar with being stuck in her room and finishing school online, was able to adapt much more easily than most. She used her spare time to create playlists, make a list of all the movies she wanted to watch, and take long walks in the empty streets with Buddy.

She was also able to take dance classes online – the seeds of which had been planted the previous summer, when she attended a musical theater camp, Broadway Bootcamp, in New York City. She'd been awarded a scholarship to the camp, making it hard to say no. Also, our friends at CF California Winemasters found out about it and helped cover the cost of our accommodations. Her days involved voice and singing classes, dance, and choreography, as well as theater and acting classes. The instructors were all Broadway performers, which made it even more exciting. She had stayed in touch with them and continued to take their classes online during lockdown. She also found online yoga classes and discovered that The Den was offering online meditation.

When most people were struggling to find ways to occupy their time, GR and I were fortunate to have plenty of creative outlets at our disposal. One initiative was the development of a mental health app for youth with life-threatening conditions, specifically CF, in hospital settings. We had already met with healthcare and tech providers in San Francisco, as well as people locally. CHLA had introduced us to their tech development team and their pain management group. We decided to use the lockdown to try to gather as many resources as possible to share GR's vision and the concept she had created.

The money raised from our last fundraiser would partially finance it. We had been recommended to an app development group in Santa Monica. We liked the fact that it was local and woman-owned. They sent us a proposal for a six- week development outline that would include bi-weekly team meetings and result in a prototype and pitch deck. We could begin, they said, once we placed the deposit.

It was a little unsettling, once we did start, to learn the actual work would be done not by local women but a team of six men from several different countries. We moved ahead anyway.

Part of the process was creating a focus group of people with CF who would provide feedback. GR started sharing on Instagram and her Foundation page about the app and the opportunity to try out a prototype and answer questions. As an added bonus, each participant would receive a twenty-five-dollar Visa gift card. We wanted them to take it seriously and provide as much insight as possible. While we found a few people with CF to participate, there were several teenagers and young adults who reached out asking why it was only for people with CF. They too were struggling with mental health issues, particularly now with the pandemic. We decided to open the focus group to all youth and young adults ages twelve to twenty-four. When we reviewed the feedback, the most fascinating were responses to the meditation questions, asking what their thoughts were on it and if they had ever practiced it. The answers ranged from, "That's too religious" to "It's for old people" or "It seems like witchcraft"!

Clearly, we had a new challenge: to find ways to engage people in short, simple breathing or walking meditations. GR asked a few of her friends who were actors or influencers to send a one-minute voiceover of some of the meditations, hoping this could be an appeal. Specific imagery, shared playlists, and positive quotes or affirmations would be included. When the prototype and deck were complete, we discovered we'd have to raise a lot more money to launch and maintain the app. This continues to evolve.

Another unfinished creative project was a children's coloring book, *Hospital Heroes,* that we wanted to publish. GR had always loved dolls. Her first, gifted to her by one of my aunts when she was eighteen months, was a Madame Alexander doll that GR promptly named Sandesta. Sandesta came everywhere with us, with GR carefully choosing her wardrobe to match the particular occasion. At restaurants, she'd even ask for a chair to be brought over for her. When she was three years old, Mom took us to the lovely restaurant, Daniel, in New York City. GR was overjoyed when the waiter brought over an ottoman for Sandesta without her even having to ask. Of course, she had no idea it was intended for our handbags! On another occasion at Geoffrey's, a restaurant in Malibu overlooking the ocean, GR had Sandesta perched on the ledge near our table to show her the view. When Sandesta accidentally slipped off and fell to the beach below, no fewer than three waiters jumped over to "rescue" her, recognizing the absolute distress GR was in. This doll was, without a doubt, like her own child.

When she got a little older, GR discovered American Girl dolls. We took her to the store in Chicago during a trip to see her godparents and grabbed an issue of their magazine, also named *American Girl.* She was fascinated. There was also a location at The Grove in Los Angeles, which I consciously tried to avoid. They were so expensive. By this time, though, we were subscribed to the magazine.

GR anticipated each issue; when it arrived, she would carefully browse the pages, marking off items for her "wish list." When she was five years old, a friend who had several AG dolls and was aware of GR's obsession, offered to give her "Kit," one of her dolls that had lost an arm. GR was thrilled. We found out that The Grove store had a hospital and took her in. We were told the operation would cost quite a bit of money and could take at least a week because Kit would need to be flown back to Wisconsin for this operation. I believed we were paying for her flight! I was relieved when GR decided that was too long to be away from her doll and that she could live without the arm.

On GR's tenth birthday, she was finally gifted a new American Girl doll customized to look like her. She cried with excitement. She took such good care of all her dolls, constantly combing through second-hand stores in search of doll clothes or furniture. In third grade, she saw a newspaper article showcasing the popularity of the AG doll. When she noticed that none of them represented a child with a disability, she decided to write a letter, accompanied by a PowerPoint presentation, to the company. She sent examples of a doll with CF, attaching photos of a medical vest, machine, and nebulizer that could be sold with it.

She agonized over each word of this four-page letter, hoping it would garner their attention. I managed to find their address and mail it. I wasn't really expecting a response but encouraged her, nonetheless. A few weeks later, a large envelope arrived from AG's corporate headquarters. We excitedly opened it to discover a message from their legal team, explaining that they were not allowed to share outside ideas with anyone in the company because it could result in legal disputes if a concept had already been in process. However, they also sent resources for how we could make our own doll and even toy companies that might assist. The last thing I needed at this moment was to start a new company, but we saved the letter.

A while later, GR and I came up with an idea for a cartoon, *Hospital Heroes*, to be shown in children's hospitals. It was sparked by a friend of ours who, when watching GR do her treatments, would always say "You're my superhero!" We thought that dolls representing these characters could subsequently be sold in the hospital gift shops. When we mentioned this to a friend who works on an animated TV show, he suggested we create a book first to acquire the intellectual property.

That's how *Hospital Heroes* the coloring book was born. We hired a graphic designer to help create the images based on GR's sketches of the characters. Each one had his or her own story about their condition and a superpower it gave them. Several characters were based on people we personally knew, including GR's close friend, who she'd met via social media, with an inoperable brain tumor, as well as a close family friend with Type 1 diabetes. The Hospital Heroes' mission, which was loosely based on GR's experience freshman year, was to fight off bullies in the outside world and teach those bullies an important lesson.

The coloring book also included a glossary at the end with more advanced terms and their explanations. The idea was that kids could learn while coloring, instead of having to do homework in the hospital. Coloring helps soothe anxiety, and we considered this the "precursor" to the app for teens. By the end of 2020 we had finished, published, and donated *Hospital Heroes* coloring books and crayons to children's hospitals around the country. It was a more sophisticated version of what we had previously gifted each Thanksgiving.

In the meantime, the pandemic had resulted in the shutdown of our factory; all our orders had either been placed "on hold" or canceled altogether. I, like many others during this time, was uncertain of my job and future. This was extremely stressful, yet I also realized how close to burnout I had come after twenty-five years in the fashion industry. It had consumed a significant portion of my mind and thoughts for most of my life, including dreaming about it throughout my youth. I was really bothered by the amount of waste in the fashion industry as a whole. It was also becoming more disrupted by the influencer-as-designer mentality.

GR's senior year was approaching and college apps were all-consuming. I was mentally preparing for a move to New York and realized it was time for a career change as well.

Stepping away from the fashion industry would create more space to welcome fresh ideas, set new goals, and pursue meaningful life work.

This felt overwhelming, terrifying, and exhilarating all at once. I wasn't sure what I would do in New York or what might be available for me as work opportunities. It had always been a life goal for me to write a book. I wasn't exactly sure what kind of book I would write; it was simply a goal. Now it was becoming clearer that perhaps I had a story to tell.

I felt like it could be cathartic.

Our Spin on a Kebab Plate

These are favorites from a variety of Greek, Persian, Mediterranean, and Asian restaurants that GR ordered from during the pandemic.

Teriyaki Chicken or Salmon kebabs over rice, Garlic Dip with Pita and Shirazi salad.

Ingredients:

- 1 lb. (450 g) chicken breast or thighs, cut into 1-inch cubes
- 1/4 cup (60 ml) soy sauce
- 2 tbsp honey (or brown sugar)
- 1 tbsp sesame oil
- 1 tbsp rice vinegar (or lemon juice)
- 2 garlic cloves, minced
- 1 tsp fresh ginger, grated
- Sesame seeds and chopped scallions (optional, for garnish)
- Skewers (soaked in water for 30 minutes if wooden)

Instructions:

1. Make the marinade:

   In a bowl, whisk together soy sauce, honey, sesame oil, rice vinegar, garlic, and ginger.

2. Marinate the chicken:

   Add the chicken pieces to the marinade. Cover and let it sit in the fridge for at least 30 minutes (or up to 2 hours for more flavor).

3. Prepare the skewers:

Add the marinated chicken onto the skewers.

4. Cook the kebabs:
   - Grill method: Preheat your grill to medium-high heat. Place the skewers on the grill and cook for 10-15 minutes, turning occasionally, until the chicken is cooked through.
   - Oven method: Preheat your oven to 425°F (220°C). Place the skewers on a baking sheet lined with foil and bake for 15-20 minutes, flipping halfway through.

1. Garnish and serve:

Sprinkle with sesame seeds and scallions. Serve warm with rice.

Garlic Dip and Pita (Purchase your favorite brands. Warm the pita.)

Salad:
Instructions:

1. Prepare:

Dice the cucumbers, tomatoes, and onion into small, even pieces.

2. Combine in a bowl:

Add the diced cucumbers, tomatoes, onion, and chopped parsley or mint to a mixing bowl.

3. Make the dressing:

In a small bowl, whisk together olive oil, lemon or lime juice, salt, and pepper.

4. Toss the salad:

   Pour the dressing over and gently toss to combine.

5. Serve immediately or chill:

   Serve fresh or refrigerate for 15-20 minutes to allow the flavors to meld.

* Can top dishes with Mediterranean black flake sea salt, for a subtle depth in flavor

TWENTY

COLLEGE APPS – MOVING ON

Several college application essay prompts inquired about accomplishments, setbacks, or inspirations. It was up to GR to decide which aspect of her life she wanted to emphasize – a daunting task, especially when it came to CF. On the one hand, it was such a big part of her life and had led to so many wonderful things she accomplished at a very young age; on the other hand, she didn't want it to define her. The concern was similar to that of the theater auditions throughout her school years: she didn't want it to deter administrators or judges from choosing her.

It was clear that she was walking a very fine line between being a good student who loved theater and had extracurricular activities that "give back," and someone who has endured, and continues to overcome, such huge, ongoing obstacles. She'd be sure to include how her future would involve becoming a very supportive alumni, hoping they would recognize her zest for the future as opposed to the fact that she may not have one.

Here were a few examples...

Essay prompt:

"Tell us something we wouldn't otherwise know about you..."

Answer #1

I was born with Cystic Fibrosis. I do daily medical treatments and take up to forty pills per day. CF is a life-threatening, life-shortening disease with no known cure. Of all the pills I take each day, that one is the hardest one to swallow.

"Why the arts?"

Answer #2:

I was born with Cystic Fibrosis, a life-threatening disease that attacks the internal organs. I take several medications daily and do hour-long treatments. My life expectancy was originally about the age I am now; however, due to scientific research and medical advancements I expect to live a full life. I was introduced to musical theater the summer before kindergarten as a creative outlet. I was hooked. This allowed me to transform into someone else. It felt like a drug, the first one that wasn't medically prescribed. I continued performing in at least two productions a year until March of 2020. Solitude helped me find a new creative outlet to get through what seemed like an eternity. I turned to writing make-believe worlds to find an escape from the one I was currently living in. I continued applying to colleges for Theater in hopes the world of Performing Arts would return to normal soon. One month later I wrote, directed, and edited my first short film and found my new prescription.

"Have you ever had to overcome any obstacles?"

Answer #3:

Since I was born, I've experienced several unpredictable circumstances. Understanding what it means to live with Cystic Fibrosis, being uprooted from my home in New Orleans due to Hurricane Katrina, having my father disappear at that same time, and having a series of unfortunate events displace my high school years. In each situation, I have found a positive way to move through it. Advocacy and public speaking on behalf of CF led me to start a Foundation to support the community. My move from New Orleans to Los Angeles fueled my love for theater and filmmaking. My father's disappearance has shown me what love and responsibility truly represent. It also provides several opportunities for future storytelling (Thank you, "Dad.") My high school experience took a toll on my mental health and encouraged me to create a coping app for teens. And of course, Covid, which helped me divert my creative outlets and find my voice in filmmaking. I am certain life will continue to present unpredictable circumstances. The privilege of this degree will help me turn them into meaningful, storytelling outcomes. I believe, in this way, I could make your institution proud.

One of the requirements when GR started at the private high school was for both of us to meet with the college counselor. The idea was for them to learn where she envisioned herself attending college and create a clear educational plan to help her meet that objective. At our first meeting, GR told them that she wanted to go to New York City and named a couple of specific schools. Their response was to ask her about safety schools, advise her to be more "realistic," and tell her to focus on schools in California.

For a second I just sat there, taken completely aback. They knew nothing about my daughter, yet they were already advising her to not only change her goals but lower her belief in herself! Completely unacceptable.

I told them what a talented and driven student she was. That she had a clothing line sold in major department stores and started a non-profit organization that had helped raise over half a million dollars for Cystic Fibrosis; that she was an advocate for Children's Hospital Los Angeles, where she was also a patient, and an advocate for the Make-A-Wish Foundation, of which she was also a recipient. She had also been acting since kindergarten and adored theater, especially Broadway. Her dream had always been to go to school in New York, which she'd visited several times and loved.

"Now, let's focus on helping her get there."

This wasn't so much about bragging about GR, but to let them know how much they didn't know. I have no objection to California schools. I know they are some of the best in the country and much more affordable to state residents. However, I'd also always been a big proponent of leaving your hometown or state for college, if you can. It gives you different perspectives on people, culture, and education.

Needless to say, I was very disappointed that the advisor didn't take the time to actually get to know students outside of a report card – and that rather than encouraging and helping them pursue their dreams, they would try to divert them from doing so.

When Grace-Rose started her sophomore year at the large public high school, she was also introduced to a counselor to help keep her on a course to meet her college goals. I was not in this meeting, but the way GR explained it to me it had gone down almost the same way. At this point, she began to disregard the assistance of her college advisors. However, halfway through her junior year at the Independent Learning Academy, I asked if they had a college advisor we could consult. I mainly wanted to ensure she met all the necessary requirements to attend college outside of California.

Many of the students in this particular ILA school program were working in entertainment, and not all of them had plans to go to college, particularly out of state, where the high school graduate requirements were different. When they introduced another college counselor for her to meet with, we simply named the schools in New York she wanted to go to. She was not considering any others, though a safety school was already recruiting her. We didn't want advice on schools, we were just making sure the requirements were met.

This very young man interjected, saying he had never heard of three of the schools she had mentioned. He also did not know Grace-Rose or anything about her and was only looking at her transcripts from three different high schools.

"I went to a school called Laverne," he said, "and it's a great school. Perhaps you should consider it or a community college here in Los Angeles."

I simply said thank you and we left. Clearly, I would have to hire, and pay quite a bit of money for, a professional college advisor. We found someone who was familiar with her schools, their academic requirements, and the performing arts community. For a variety of reasons, her high school had been so disrupted that we wanted to make sure she was on the right course. It was also helpful to have a second set of eyes reading her essays and offering suggestions.

Grace-Rose had always been on top of her education, incredibly organized, and aware of deadlines – and this time was no different. She had compiled a list of her schools, along with their requirements, and had files for each, along with the dates marked on her calendar as to when these applications would open. What made the application process more intense than most was that in addition to the usual transcripts, resumes, and essays, she had to audition as well. The auditions might include singing, dance, monologues, a portfolio, and a scheduled interview. The frustrating part was that due to Covid, none would be done in person, which she prefers.

During the pandemic, and its disruption of live entertainment, she had witnessed entertainers being forced to pivot. Many began writing. Now, she was realizing that the schools she was applying to, particularly the NYU theater school, were heavily focused on getting students to Broadway. She became a little uncertain; though she would love to continue acting and dancing, including on the stage, she also wanted options other than Broadway. After finishing the entire application and audition process, she decided at the last minute to switch to a program at NYU that would allow her to create her own career objectives. We were both hesitant about this, as the curriculum didn't seem to be quite the right fit; however, not having a film or TV portfolio and that being her only other real interest, she went along with this application anyway.

As any applicant knows, the anticipation of decisions is unnerving. It's extremely exciting when acceptance letters arrive, particularly if they include some sort of scholarship. When those letters came, GR was instantly and immensely relieved, knowing that she would have the option of going to New York to study performing arts with a scholarship attached. She did not get accepted to NYU, and while this certainly upset her, it confirmed her gut feeling that the department she'd applied for wasn't the right fit. And, while she regretted not continuing the application for the theater department, she wouldn't have been able to transfer out of it had she been accepted, and she knew she wanted more.

Of the wonderful options she had, she chose The New School for Performing Arts. It was also serendipitous because the first fashion program I did during one summer in high school was at Parsons School of Design, which is part of The New School. While I ultimately attended FIT for college, this certainly felt like a full-circle moment. TNS has wonderful schools and programs, so it seemed like the right decision.

One day, we were driving around Burbank, looking for a place for my father to move. He was leaving Boston and wanted to be in California, near family. He also wanted to be near a tennis club, so we were looking in the Toluca Lake neighborhood adjacent to Burbank and home to the Toluca Lake Tennis Club, of which he would soon become a member.

We stopped at a famous old diner called Bob's Big Boy to grab a snack from their takeout window. As we were waiting for the food we both glanced at the bright pink building on the corner called Milt & Edie's. It also happened to be across the street from the office I had rented so GR could go to the school in Burbank. We saw it all the time, commenting on how it looked like it should be an ice cream shop or old-school diner rather than a dry cleaner. Apparently, it's been around forever, catering to all the wardrobe departments in the nearby studios, like Disney, Warner Brothers, and Paramount. As we stood there talking about the dry cleaner, I noticed for the first time the four-story brick building next to it. It said Laverne University – the same school her last college counselor had recommended to her. When I pointed it out to GR, we both started laughing. It wasn't because anything was wrong with it, but had she listened to him, her dreams of school in NYC would have been squashed.

Lox & Bagels – Our "go-to" bagel in NYC

Tal Bagel, close to our NY apartment serves them; they also have some of my favorite black & white cookies.

Traditional: Use an Everything Bagel

California taco style:
Use Street Tacos – melt a little butter in a skillet with Everything But the Bagel seasoning and place tacos in to get the everything bagel flavor.

Add these ingredients to either the traditional or taco style:

    Regular or Chive Cream Cheese

    Sliced Nova Lox salmon

    Sliced Red Onion

    Sliced Tomato

    Dill

    Capers

* For a saltier flavor, use Caper berries

TWENTY-ONE

NEW YORK CITY – TRANSITIONS

I was nineteen years old sitting with my roommate, Amy, on the steps of my dorm at FIT on 27th Street in Manhattan. I remember seeing this tall guy walking across the street with another shorter guy. There was something about his confident strut and effortless smile. He was wearing long denim shorts, an orange terry cloth oversized polo shirt and orange and white shell-toe Adidas to match. An unusual thing about me is that I can recall just about anything with the memory of an outfit, and I clearly recall thinking that this person was going to have some impact on my life. In fact, he did, perhaps the most significant.

Years later, on one of our trips to New York, when GR was still fairly young but old enough to understand, I would take her to these steps and tell her that story. I always wanted her to feel comfortable talking about her father, if she wanted to. I also always wanted her to know just how much she was meant to be here, regardless of his actions.

Thirty years later, my daughter was starting college in New York City. Another one of life's full- circle moments.

* * *

At the time, GR was still having anxiety and going to therapy for it.

She took buses as opposed to subways, always texting me her where-abouts, having me follow her locations, looking for exits, not going out late, etc. I had become accustomed to this and if she didn't receive an immediate reply it would concern her. Other times, when we were together, she'd suddenly stop me and, her face flushing, say, "Mom, I'm starting to get anxious. Feel my heart, it's racing."

It would come unexpectedly out of nowhere, even if she was in a "safe space." She would try to take deep breaths but couldn't, which would then escalate into her not being able to breathe and generate concerns about her CF lungs. It didn't matter what I said or how much I tried to calm her or ask her what she was thinking about or where she thought these feelings were coming from. There was nothing I could do but stand with her and wait.

Once it subsided, she'd apologize for ruining a moment or rushing us out of somewhere. I have to admit, at times it was inconvenient, particularly if we were with other people, but I would also apologize, mainly for not being able to help.

She said to me one time, "I think it would be more helpful if you didn't say anything at all and just hugged me."

Well, that I could definitely do.

Anxiety and panic attacks are not something I fully understand; however, there were a few occasions, when my mom was in the midst of all her medical emergencies, when I believed I was experiencing these feelings. This made it a little bit easier for me to relate.

It was also another reason for me to stay close. I didn't want GR's college experience and life to be consumed by these thoughts. Therapy was helpful, but it wasn't a cure, and I was determined to help her move through it in any way I could.

The start of this transitional year consisted of disappointing Air-bnbs, generous friends offering their homes, and several hotel stays with and without Buddy as I searched for an apartment in New York. In between, there were flights to and from New Orleans, where my sister was taking care of Buddy for us.

In the meantime, GR was going through her own major transition: she had moved into her dorm, and for the first time, was living away from me and Buddy. She was in a suite with four roommates, but she had a single room – something she arranged so her noisy treatments wouldn't disturb anyone. She had carefully chosen a close friend from L.A., who she knew from her performing arts middle school, to be one of her suitemates. I was still managing the majority of her medical needs so the transition wouldn't overwhelm her and her health wouldn't be compromised in the process. I ordered refills, dealt with insurance, set up doctor visits, and booked flights for quarterly clinics back in L.A. Knowing this, and the fact that we were nearby, provided her some level of comfort.

She would frequently stop by my hotel after classes, take Buddy for walks, come look at apartments with me, or join me for dinner. She also knew after the first few weeks of classes that this was not the right program for her. It was reminiscent of high school, when she knew after the first day that the private school had been the wrong choice. It was beginning to depress her. Her suitemate and friend from home, who had a similar background in performing arts, felt the same way – that it was remedial and uninspiring. They were learning nothing and had zero motivation.

GR reached out to the administration to see if she could enroll in a more advanced program, but they informed her that these were all prerequisites and therefore non-negotiable. I would listen in on some of her Zoom classes (in-person classes had not completely resumed) and could attest to the reason for her indifference. Some of our friends and family members explained that this was what freshman year was like – you have to repeat work and just get used to college life. Perhaps, but in this case I disagreed. One of the worst things any motivated student can encounter is boredom. More importantly, I know my child. This wasn't just a new, challenging situation – GR had encountered plenty of those – this was an actual problem. She believed she was wasting time, something that had always been very precious to her. She also felt it was a waste of money – a lot of it – and I agreed.

We both tried speaking to different administrators, including deans and even the school president. We weren't trying to diminish the program, just simply trying to find one that was a better fit, but it seemed we couldn't find a resolution. Going to school in New York had been a dream her whole life, and to see it going this way – and seeing her so down – was weighing on me. To make matters worse, her suitemate, who had become similarly depressed, left after two months and returned to L.A. At least Buddy and I were nearby, so that helped get her through it.

We came up with a strategy – push through freshman year, make plans to look forward to, and apply to transfer to another school. GR was afraid this association would forever tarnish her feelings for New York, so we made efforts to do and see things all over the city and outskirts that we hadn't before. She would walk different ways to school, try a new coffee shop each day, create a Taco Tuesday night in her dorm, take an online film course, anything to "look forward to" and of course, spend whatever free time she could with Buddy. When we returned to L.A. for doctors' visits and clinics she would feverishly work on building a film portfolio with her best friend, who had previously been filming projects with her. During covid, they had created a few short films and written a few scripts and TV pilots together, so this wasn't completely new to her. When she realized Broadway and musical theater may not be the end-all be-all for her, she had developed a larger appreciation for film and TV. She decided she was going to reapply to NYU for Tisch's Film and TV production degree.

I, on the other hand, was trying to figure out what my "third quarter" was going to be. I look at life as consisting of four quarters, like a basketball game. By fifty, you're at the half, next is your third quarter. Some call it a "second mountain." As my fiftieth birthday approached, I realized I had never had this much time and space, particularly in my head, to consider anything outside the world of fashion. What do you do when your entire life has been consumed with a career and career goals, only to have that disappear, almost overnight? I would explain it to friends as though ninety percent of my brain was occupied with these thoughts and now they were freed up. It was the strangest feeling.

I had experience in events, having hosted so many fashion fundraisers and freelancing at times with two of my closest friends in L.A., who had large event companies. One specialized in weddings and film premieres, the other in sports and entertainment. I found two other events companies, one in New York and one in New Orleans, that I would begin freelancing with as well. This would also allow me to travel alone, something I hadn't done in twenty years.

I considered a concept for a new boutique I wanted to open, but I was conflicted. I was new-ish to NY and felt I had a bigger network in either New Orleans or Los Angeles to support a new store. I also wasn't sure how long we'd be staying in New York. If GR wasn't going to stay in school there I didn't want to be committed to a lengthy retail lease. I also had a food and beverage concept, as well as real estate concepts that I thought could work in any one of these cities, but again, wasn't sure which place I'd end up. While in the limbo space, I would attend networking events, CFF events, and a series of workshops in order to meet new people and develop potential work opportunities.

I could also continue working with Grace-Rose's foundation, focusing on fundraising and raising awareness for Cystic Fibrosis, while continuing to develop the app. However, I didn't want to involve GR, as she was transitioning to a new environment and gaining independence. I didn't want her to feel consumed by or committed to this. She was trying to find her new identity, as was I, and this meant allowing her that space. If I were to continue the work with her foundation, it would have to be alone, at least for now.

This, along with events, would occupy my time. I decided it was time to start writing my book.

Steak Frites

I first took GR to Pastis NYC when she was three years old. I still have the framed, colorful picture she drew for me on the back of the menu. She fell in love with steak frites.

Ingredients

- Steak: 2 ribeye or sirloin steaks (about 1-inch thick)
- Salt and black pepper, to taste
- 2 tbsp butter
- 2 cloves garlic, smashed
- Fresh thyme or rosemary (optional)
- Frites: 2 large russet potatoes
- Vegetable oil (for frying)
- Salt, to taste

Instructions

1. Prepare the Fries:
   - Cut potatoes into thin strips and soak in water for 20-30 minutes. Drain and pat dry.
   - Heat oil to 350°F (175°C) and fry potatoes in batches until golden and crispy. Drain on paper towels and season with salt.

2. Cook the Steak:
   - Season steaks with salt and pepper. In a hot skillet, add butter, garlic, and herbs. Sear steaks for 3-4 minutes per side, basting with melted butter until your desired doneness.

*For a smoky steak flavor, finish with a touch of Maldon Smoked Sea Salt.

*For a "richer and saltier" French fry experience top with Creme fraiche and Caviar

TWENTY-TWO

LOSS – BUDDY

W hen it was time to move GR into her dorm at TNS, we had been staying at a nearby boutique hotel in Gramercy. We mapped out plans to go to Bed Bath and Beyond, Target, and Marshall's for dorm necessities and accessories. We were trying to figure out the logistics of it in the city and with public transportation. In the middle of all this, we received notification from the school that some of the covid test results had not come back yet, meaning that several students would not be able to move into the dorm on the dates and times planned. This was frustrating and unsettling as the anticipation of move-in was looming.

While we were making a list of things to pick up, I got a call from my close friend Laura in L.A., who had gone to check our mail and water our plants.

"I think somebody may have broken into your home," she said, then told me she had found the door ajar, the lock looking like it had been tampered with.

Laura then Facetimed me and walked me through the rooms. I sighed in relief when I saw that nothing in the front of the home appeared to have been touched.

Then she got to my bedroom…

It had been completely torn apart. All the jewelry with monetary or sentimental value — gold pieces my mom had given me from my grandmother, including charm bracelets commemorating significant events — had been hidden in a purse inside another bag, tucked under a robe in the back closet. I was waiting until I had settled on a place to live in New York to bring it, rather than keeping it in hotels. It was all gone.

The drawers had also been rifled through; their contents, including GR's NICU hospital photos and novelties, were now strewn across the floor. Other keepsakes from her baby years – a sterling silver rattle and tiny jade and gold bracelets – had been taken. Also missing was the considerable amount of cash I had hidden in a drawer at the suggestion of a friend to keep some on hand during covid. GR's room and my mother's room had been torn apart as well.

I stared at the phone, stunned, then at the mess. I felt sad, helpless, and violated, all at once.

Immediately, I knew this was an inside job. The building was very secure, with two gated entries; plus, our condo was in the front, with lots of passersby all day. All stolen items were easy to exit with – nothing large like electronics – and to find these hidden items the thief would have had to have ample time to go through things without fear of being discovered. The unit behind ours was being renovated and I remembered the workmen watching us leave with several large pieces of luggage. They had probably watched as two of my friends had entered around the same time each day to water plants and check mail. Last but not least, the burglary had taken place on the last day of construction. Clearly, this had been orchestrated. There was nothing I could do other than call the police; my friends waited for them to come so they could file a police report and take fingerprints. This would result in nothing.

It was all I could do to remain positive, the goal being to get GR comfortable as she moved into the dorm. Inside, though I felt gutted.

The burglary was immediately followed by another shock. After getting her settled at school, we went to check into the Airbnb in Chelsea, where I would stay for the next month while apartment hunting. It had taken months of searching to find this unit — which, I now realized, looked nothing like the photos. The sparseness was disappointing, but far worse was the lack of cleanliness, including molded food in the microwave, smelly enough to permeate the entire unit. The bathroom pipes made loud noises when I turned on the shower, disturbing not only me but the alcoholic neighbor below who banged on the pipes, then my front door.

We contacted Airbnb immediately. I had already bought cleaning supplies and started cleaning it myself because I was exhausted, depleted, and had no place else to go. They wanted to send plumbers in and a cleaning crew, which was all disconcerting as we were still dealing with Covid. Leaving the apartment while they worked was not an option; I wasn't about to leave my belongings unattended, especially after being burglarized.

Suddenly, I was scrambling to find a new place to stay while searching for an apartment. I tried booking another Airbnb, only to be charged $5,900 for a place I hadn't even stayed in. Attempts to reach their customer service went nowhere. It was a disaster and another financial loss. After a weeklong stay at a friend's place in Midtown, I managed to find a reasonable hotel in NoMad. Thankfully, Buddy was staying with my sister Kate in New Orleans, so I didn't have to consider "dog-friendly" options or subject him to the upheaval.

We were so grateful to Kate for the help, and she was thrilled to have a youthful companion for their older pug, Miles. Then, just a few weeks after we moved to New York, she called to tell us that Miles had passed away.

This was incredibly sad. Miles was GR's first introduction to pugs – actually, her introduction to dogs – and she always looked forward to New Orleans visits for sleepovers and cuddles with him. He was special. After we found out, we were walking silently in Chelsea, taking in the weight of the news. At that very moment, we passed a small, unexpected cemetery and a lady with a pug walked by. It felt like a farewell from Miles.

For nearly two months I would continue to bounce between Los Angeles, New Orleans, and New York. Has the process of getting an apartment in New York become more frustrating over the years, or had I simply forgotten after so much time away? I didn't know, and it didn't matter - either way, I was utterly exhausted.

One day, I got a call from GR, who had been looking for me as well.

"Just sign the lease papers," she said after telling me about the place she'd found, "and trust me."

I did trust her, but I also knew that if I didn't snatch it up at that moment, it would be gone.

Within two days, Buddy and I were back in New York and moving into the new apartment.

Though GR and I had visited New York countless times, it was so strange to be moving back. The last time I had lived there it was with a youthful, hopeful effervescence of beginning my career in fashion – my lifelong dream. Now I was returning after leaving a long career in fashion and trying to discover a whole new version of myself. It felt as though my identity was lost.

In fact, another piece of that identity would soon fall away. The condo we rented in L.A. was being put up for sale, and we had to be out in thirty days. I flew to California to pack up over two decades of belongings – mine, GR's, and Mom's. We donated several boxes to charity and a warehouse full of brand-new Rosie G clothes to The Watts Community Center, where Children Mending Hearts was orchestrating a "back to school" gifting. Whatever valuables we had left went into storage. It was a monumental amount of work, done in the short space of a month. In the process I would lose a package with several sentimental items that were FedExed to me in New York and never arrived. I also lost a gift, given to me for Grace-Rose when she was young, to be opened on her twenty-first birthday. Everything was beginning to feel like too much. What was the Universe trying to tell me?

Added to this was Grace-Rose's disappointment with school. As always, she combatted a miserable situation by doubling down, spending every moment of free time creating a film and screenwriting portfolio to use when she reapplied to NYU for Film & TV production. Her "back-up" plan – returning to Los Angeles and trying to work in the film business with her friends – was not a desirable one.

She wanted a college degree and she desperately wanted to be in New York. I did too – and I had just signed a year lease. I wasn't sure what I would do if she didn't return to school sophomore year.

Before we knew it, the end of her freshman year was approaching. She had sent in her application to NYU and now all we could do was wait. To shift focus and relieve stress, we channeled our efforts into other creative things, one of them being the app that we had been working on for two years.

We occasionally took meetings or calls together regarding grants or philanthropic associations for youth and mental health. Someone had introduced us to a psychiatrist who was an NYU graduate and a young woman starting a youth mental health website for psychiatry. We thought it could be a good collaboration and set up a Zoom meeting for April 11.

On this day, Grace-Rose debated whether to return to her dorm after class to shower and change or go directly to my place uptown for the meeting. She decided to come uptown to spend more time with Buddy. As soon as she arrived, he ran to the front door, whimpering in excitement and jumping on her. He always greeted her this way when she walked in the door, even if she just stepped outside to throw out the trash. He was always incredibly happy to see her and would leap into her arms or her lap.

She had begged me for a pug for years, ever since she'd met and fallen in love with Miles. I wasn't sure how I could care for another being, financially or physically. GR finally won me over at the age of twelve when she said, "Mom, pugs have breathing issues just like me, so we can relate."

I melted.

That Christmas, tucked into a watermelon clutch bag (GR loved Watermelons), she found a note with a picture of a baby pug that was hers. We had already planned a Klump trip to Washington, D.C., so we'd have to wait until our return to pick him up. She could hardly contain her excitement. They would become inseparable.

We were sitting at the table together, preparing notes for the call. I was explaining a little bit about the person we were meeting with so GR would have a better idea of some questions to ask. We had the computer pulled up, open and ready.

Buddy was resting in her lap per usual. About five minutes before the call started, GR suddenly said, "Mom, something's wrong with Buddy." She yelled, "Something's wrong!" and jumped up. He felt heavier all of a sudden.

I looked across the table and couldn't understand what was happening, but I trusted her and rushed to look up the closest veterinary ER. He then let out a small whimper and his tongue fell out of his mouth. She raced to the door. My hand was shaking as I was dialing. We were running down the steps; she was hysterical.

"I think he's dying," she said as he defecated and went limp in her arms. We ran to the corner and pushed a couple aside who had just hailed a cab.

"My dog is dying!" she cried, and they jumped out of the way. We pleaded with the driver to take us to 64th and 2nd Avenue as quickly as possible. Never, in all my time in Manhattan, had I had such a slow driver. When we realized he wasn't going to go any faster, we told him to pull over, we jumped out, I threw cash into the front seat, and we jumped in another cab.

This driver understood the urgency. As he sped toward the veterinary ER, I kept telling GR to talk to Buddy, tell him we need him to stay with us, it was not his time to go.

In utter distress, she cried, "Please, please Buddy, don't leave me. I need you!"

Traffic was insufferable; we had two blocks to go. I told GR we needed to get out and start running. I asked her to let me hold him and I'd run as fast as I could. She said, "No, I'm not letting him go," as we raced to the vet. They knew we were coming, I had called to let them know. When we arrived the doctors had the doors wide open, rushing him inside to begin CPR. I watched at least four vets performing CPR on him. Grace-Rose couldn't. She just kept looking at me for some sort of reassurance from behind the doors.

I stood inside watching, as now, seven doctors were involved – intubating him, giving him shots, and performing CPR. After ten minutes the lead doctor came out and said, "The maximum amount of time we can perform CPR is twelve minutes. What would you like us to do?"

GR turned the corner, scared to look, and with tears in her eyes, cried, "Don't stop, please don't stop."

The doctor, knowing Buddy was already gone, returned and performed CPR for three more minutes, past the time they were allowed. She came out and said, "I'm so sorry, we did everything we could."

GR and I burst into tears. I couldn't tell if I was weeping more for Buddy or Grace-Rose. It was a combination of shock and disbelief. It was such a sudden and unexpected death. They brought us into a room and said we could sit with him and mourn for as long as we needed. She held him in her arms, crying desperately, hoping it was all a nightmare. The vet was incredible. She came in and sat on the floor next to us; she told GR that this very same thing had happened to her when she was young. It's what made her choose to become a vet. She could tell Buddy was a very important member of our family.

It was tragic and unbelievable and, after the year we'd had, I didn't know how much more loss we could handle. Her best friend and support was gone. We knew we couldn't stay with him all night because the doctor reminded us he would get stiffer and colder in her arms and it's not the way she would want to remember him. We decided we would leave when his feeding alarm – the sound of a bark – on her phone went off. When that alarm went off, we both just looked at each other, looked at Buddy, and started to weep all over again. The doctor came in and took him, and I can't even recall the walk home. When we got back, she just sat on the sofa in the T-shirt he had urinated on and wouldn't move. For people who have never had pets, it's difficult to describe the joy and unconditional love they offer, or the magnitude of the loss when they pass away. I truly didn't know how I could help her navigate this grief.

Of everything we had faced, this tragic, unexpected loss was by far the hardest.

On that same day, randomly, my Instagram and Facebook accounts were hacked and locked. That felt like another loss of connectivity. Meta was impossible to contact and I had no energy to deal with it. It would take months to revive. It would also take me two weeks to get Grace-Rose out of bed. All she could do was look at pictures and videos of Buddy, cry in the shower, and try to sleep. I had to write to her professors at school to allow her to finish the last two weeks online, which she managed to do.

Finally, I convinced her to come outside. I knew she needed fresh air; plus, I had found a place that had puppies for adoption and I thought the only thing that might make her smile would be to play with some. We walked through Central Park to the West Side in silence. There was nothing to say.

When we entered the shop, they brought out a baby black French bulldog who instantly fell in love with her. He started licking her face and climbing all over her, reminding her of Buddy, but also making her giggle. I was so relieved to see a smile return to her face. Afterward, when we were walking back through the park to go home, a rainbow appeared in the middle of the sky out of nowhere.

GR turned to me and said, "Mom, I was feeling so guilty about playing with another puppy, but now I know that it was okay. The rainbow is Buddy's way of letting me know."

When we returned to the apartment, she opened her computer to see if there was any unfinished work she had left for school. That's when she saw the email from the NYU Tisch Film & TV school letting her know that she had been accepted. We were elated, but it was bittersweet. It was a sign from Buddy. It felt as though, with the ultimate loss, a new blessing had been found.

In less than a year, we had endured the loss of the burglary; our home in L.A.; Miles, GR's gift; the shipment; my identity in fashion; and now Buddy.

I could only imagine that perhaps the Universe was stripping us of everything so we could start anew.

Something I wish I had learned sooner in life is the practice of forgiveness. It doesn't mean we have to be okay with the person or the situation we are forgiving, but we get to let go of the dark space it's taking up inside of us. Once we forgive it, it lightens our burdens, including those we didn't even know we were carrying. It's not always easy, but it is certainly restorative.

Favorite Salads: Something light in context to the chapter

My family loves my salads, we always have one with Klump dinner.

In fact, when my nephew was very young and asked what he wanted for his birthday meal he replied "Tia Leah's salad!"

The first one is modified from the Chopped salad at Laurel Tavern in L.A., one of GR's favorites:

Chopped lettuces, crumbled bleu cheese, grilled corn, diced granny smith apples, sliced marinated red onions and champagne vinaigrette

My nephews preferred:

Red leaf and butter lettuces, arugula, and shredded cabbage with hearts of palm, garbanzo beans and colorful carrots, mandoline-style with homemade dressing: minced garlic, dijon mustard, olive oil, rice wine vinegar, sugar and salt (combine and heat in the microwave for 10 seconds) stir and toss warm dressing into salad

Spinach Salad, avocado and toasted pine nuts with Japanese dressing, one of our favorites being - Pietro's Original Shoyu Japanese dressing (found at Japanese groceries or online)

Heirloom tomatoes sliced, topped with burrata or stracciatella and drizzled with olive oil and glazed vinegar

*   Top with Portuguese floral salt (tiny flowers elevate the appearance).

TWENTY - THREE

LONDON – NEW OPPORTUNITIES

After GR's freshman year of college, full of anticipation about attending NYU in the fall, we headed west for CF California Winemasters. I had already told Barbara and DawnMarie about the loss of Buddy and how everything since had felt so heavy. GR's spirits were down, I said, and I wasn't sure she'd have her usual energetic stage presence.

GR had been doing research on pug rescues in California. She said she had "spoken to Buddy" about it and asked his permission. She assured him that nothing could ever replace him, but she couldn't stand coming home to the emptiness he had left. We found a puppy that had been abandoned and rescued by a pug rescue approximately two hours away. We called to see if he was available and if we could meet him, though I was a bit hesitant. I was still dealing with the unexpected medical bills from Buddy's ER visit and was concerned about taking on new financial and 'puppy' responsibilities. That's when I got a call from DawnMarie.

"Barbara and I have discussed this," she said, "and with your permission we'd like to gift GR a new puppy this year from her Winemasters family. We'll cover all the costs."

Hearing this and once again feeling the support of a "village," I was flooded with emotion. I called the rescue back and asked if we could visit the baby pug, to see if he and GR had a connection, and whether she was ready for him. I then mentioned the gift from Winemasters – and that it would be a surprise. If we did decide to adopt him, they would have to wait three more days for someone to arrange to pick him up prior to the event so he could be presented to GR then.

We met at a playground, and when GR picked him up, his little tail wagging, he instantly started licking the necklace she had customized with Buddy's face on it.

We looked at each other with tears in our eyes. She didn't want to let him go, but I reminded her that we were still considering it and had a lot to discuss. Plus, the rescue woman had other prospects set up to meet him. This was not entirely true, but it was the only way I could separate the two of them.

On the ride home, GR said, "I think it was a sign that he gravitated straight to my Buddy necklace. I really want to adopt him."

She was scheduled for a therapy call during the drive. I pulled over and said, "I'll walk into this coffee shop and give you some privacy in the car to take your call."

She insisted that it was fine for me to listen in, but I didn't want to. I needed to let the rescue know, as well as DawnMarie and Barbara, that we wanted to adopt him and start making arrangements.

When we returned home, GR yelled at me from her room. "Mom, come see. I prayed to Buddy to please send me a sign that this was okay."

Sure enough, there was a rainbow shining through her window right next to Buddy's urn! She pleaded with me to call the rescue back and tell them we wanted him. Of course, now I would have to stall. With three days left before the event, I wasn't sure how to handle this. I didn't want to ruin the surprise; I also didn't want to devastate her again.

The following day, she asked me again. Still stalling, I told her I had left a message. That evening, after asking me several more times, I finally said, "Sorry love, but the couple that came after us adopted him. I'm sure it's meant to be."

It broke my heart to see her so sad again but told myself that ultimately she would be thrilled with the surprise. Two whole days later, we were attending the Friday night Sponsor dinner before the big event. They had decided to surprise her here since the pup hadn't had all of his shots and couldn't be in larger crowds. Plus, this was a more intimate event, with all the big donors who had contributed to this adoption.

During the auction, when it was time to introduce GR and have her say a few words, they presented her with a large vintage Louis Vuitton bag. A little perplexed, as gifts hadn't really been part of the introduction before, she thanked the group for the very thoughtful gift and commented on how heavy it was. They urged her to open it. The minute she unzipped the purse, out popped the little pug, once again, licking her Buddy necklace and ferociously wagging his tail.

GR burst into tears, happy, grateful tears. The following night, it was almost impossible to drag her to the event with the new puppy at home. Our friend offered to bring her daughters over to play with him and keep an eye on him until we returned. On stage, during the live auction introduction with GR, they played the video from the previous night. The "Bid for the Cure" was a huge success and I saw her spark return.

She named him Cooper.

The following day, she received notice that her new introductory NYU film class would start Monday! With all the other things we had been dealing with, we'd somehow missed the part about a mandatory summer film class for transfer students. I scrambled to find us red-eye flights and make sure we had everything Coop needed.

GR had sworn to me that she'd be able to potty train and care for a new puppy with this being her first summer "off" in a long time. Now, here we were, back in New York, GR with a full class load and me having to care for this new baby.

GR loved NYU from the first day. I know Buddy was never far from her thoughts – she had somewhat of an altar dedicated to him – but I was so relieved to see her happy again. She was loving her classes, applying for summer internships, and planning for a junior year abroad. She had already done the research of NYU film programs and decided that the London advanced screenwriting course would be the perfect one for her. It was a small program, for which she would have to apply and interview. She did the same for her summer internship with a large film Production Studio in L.A. She was accepted to both. Now we had to plan to spend the summer back in L.A. for the internship and the fall in London for a semester abroad. I would have to sublet my New York apartment and find housing in London.

I also discovered that the UK doesn't allow dogs to be brought into the country, at least not without a month-long quarantine first. I would now have to find a dog sitter stateside while we were abroad.

With the help of our wonderful family and friends, we found a sub-letter in NY and a place to stay for the summer in L.A. We also found a dog sitter in New Orleans; we'd fly Coop there and acclimate him to his temporary home before heading to London.

London… where we still had no place to live, with just two weeks left before our one-way flights. Increasingly nervous, I signed GR up for a dorm and booked myself a temporary bnb. Then, a few days prior to our departure, I found a Facebook group for women-only house swappers. Chloe was looking for a London – NYC swap for a few months and I immediately reached out and arranged a meeting as soon as I arrived. We clicked right away, exchanged keys, and that was that!

I loved her place in Battersea; GR was farther away, at Tower Hill. We were close enough for emergencies but far enough to feel independent.

She was going to classes and dating; I was writing my book and planning travel.

My brother came out to celebrate my birthday and take us to dinner and to see *Cabaret*. Our family came out for Thanksgiving to travel to Amsterdam and Copenhagen.

We had weekend and holiday excursions throughout the semester, visiting places around the U.K, including Edinburgh, Glasgow, The Lake District, Bath, Bristol, Liverpool, Canterbury, Rye, Cambridge, Oxford, The Cotswolds, and Brighton Beach.

GR's twenty-first birthday was the Monday after Thanksgiving. I knew we'd be at the tail-end of our family trip and asked her if she had a preference of where she would want to wake up as a twenty-one-year-old.

She quickly replied, "Paris!"

It wasn't completely unexpected. Eight years earlier, my sister and brother-in-law had gotten married in the courtyard of the Louvre during the week of Thanksgiving. We had a family celebration for GR's thirteenth birthday at Ladurée on the Champs Elysees. She had an unforgettable crepe in Le Marais and dreamt of returning to it.

On November 26, after my family had departed, we flew from Copenhagen to Paris to spend the night. She got her wish of waking up there on her twenty-first birthday, and we returned to the little crepe shop. It was memorable, to say the least.

We took the train back to London, where I had already booked a special "high tea" and show at the National Theatre for her birthday. GR was not much of a drinker, so tea seemed like the appropriate British way to celebrate such a momentous birthday.

I also couldn't help but think that new opportunities were on the horizon.

Sunday Roast

This old UK tradition features a large portion of meat and gravy, veggies, crisp or mashed potatoes, and Yorkshire pudding, sometimes served with cheesy cauliflower and Hispi cabbage as well.

All are meant to be eaten "family style" and only served on Sundays. GR and I loved this tradition and enjoyed trying different pubs or restaurants all over the UK to rate our favorites.

She preferred the roasted chicken, while I liked the beef and I love cabbage. So does London. It's often grilled and offered as a side on many menus.

Sunday Roast felt like Thanksgiving every week!

Yorkshire Pudding
Ingredients

- 1 cup all-purpose flour
- 1 cup milk
- 3 large eggs
- 1/2 tsp salt
- 1/4 cup vegetable oil or beef drippings

Instructions

Step 1: Prepare the Batter

1. Combine Ingredients: In a mixing bowl, whisk together the flour, milk, eggs, and salt until the batter is smooth and has no lumps. Let the batter rest for 15-30 minutes (optional, but it can help the puddings rise better).

Step 2: Preheat the Oven and Muffin Tin

1. Preheat Oven: Preheat your oven to 425°F (220°C).

2. Prepare the Muffin Tin: Pour a little oil or a small piece of beef drippings (about 1/2 tsp) into each cup of a 12-cup muffin tin.

3. Heat the Oil: Place the muffin tin in the preheated oven for 5-10 minutes, or until the oil is very hot and just starting to smoke.

Step 3: Bake the Yorkshire Puddings

1. Add Batter to the Muffin Tin: Carefully remove the muffin tin from the oven and pour the batter into each cup, filling them about halfway.

2. Bake: Return the tin to the oven and bake for 15-20 minutes, or until the puddings are puffed up and golden brown. Do not open the oven during baking, as this can cause them to deflate.

Step 4: Serve

1. Serve Immediately: Yorkshire puddings are best enjoyed fresh from the oven while they're still crisp.

Choose your meat, gravy, veggies, and sides...
Enjoy with family or friends. It's meant to be a group gathering.

* Pinch any Maldon Salt, from Maldon, UK as a topping

TWENTY-FOUR

CHRISTMAS ABROAD – DISCOVERING INDEPENDENCE

If I could give her the world...

I had been planning this trip for months – reminiscent of my junior year abroad and all the magical European places I visited. I wanted GR to see as much as possible with the limited time and budget we had. My travel, thirty years earlier, had been with different groups of friends I had met abroad. Her excursions would be with me. It was not lost on me that this was unusual, but our circumstances always had been. I was flattered that she'd even consider taking this trip together; we were getting accustomed to living apart and spending more and more time away from one another.

For the most part, GR was also managing her health on her own at this point. Her medical team had allowed her to cut some of her treatments short and gave her smaller, portable devices specifically designed for travel. She was slowly weaning herself off some of the medications to see how she would feel without them. Several patients who had started taking Trikafta were discovering this as well after being on the medication for a few years. The new anxiety medication she was taking made it much easier for her to take public transportation, the tube, and trains. It also gave her a new level of comfort navigating crowds and going places alone.

Between these two miracle drugs, I was seeing a completely different child. One who would soon no longer need my constant presence. I would take full advantage of our Bon Voyage!

Our adventure consisted of four cities in Eastern Europe, four in Italy, and four in France. It was so difficult to narrow it down, but I thought these would all give her a taste of the various countries and an idea of where she might want to return or explore further. It was predominantly for the exposure.

This is how it went:

Plane to Berlin

Train to Prague

Train to Vienna

Train to Budapest

Got stuck in Austria overnight surrounded by snow capped mountains and delayed in a small town called Villach

Ended up on a bus to Venice, due to an unforeseen strike

Train to Rome (Christmas in Rome started with the Pope's mass in St. Peter's Square at the Vatican and ended with a twenty-five-person dinner with strangers at a local's home in Trastevere. The meal consisted of eight courses of traditional Italian family recipes ending with grappa, limoncello, Italian desserts, and dancing. It was our first Christmas without family, but did not disappoint.)

Train to Florence

Train to Cinque Terre (Stayed in Vernazza)

Train to Nice

Train to Monte Carlo

Train to Paris (New Year's Eve was spent at another stranger's home for a late-night dinner party in the Marais neighborhood)

Train to Strasbourg (Christmas markets were everywhere we went!)

Return to London via Paris.

We now had two days left in London before we returned to New York. We would drop off all of our luggage in NY then have to fly to New Orleans to pick up Cooper on our way to Los Angeles for her final CHLA CF clinic. They had allowed her to excuse one of her quarterly clinics since she was abroad, as long as she checked in to let them know how she was doing and whether the abbreviated treatments and meds were working.

The day before we were to leave London, GR and I went to one of the NYU dorms to retrieve the bulk of her belongings, which she had left there while we were traveling. We lugged the two large suitcases toward San Pancras, the closest tube station and one of the largest international train stations. We would take the Victoria line and transfer to the neighborhood where we were staying. As we walked, GR and I reminisced about our recent travels and what we would miss most about London, as well as what we were looking forward to back in the States.

When we arrived at the train terminal it was packed, which was common. I was a few steps ahead since it was too crowded with our large suitcases to walk side by side. There are about four train lines leaving from the same entry point. I placed my card on the turnstile to pay the entry fee and started walking toward the escalator, assuming GR was still right behind me. Once on the escalator I turned around to look for her. I didn't see her. This was odd. When I got to the bottom of the long escalator and still didn't see her, I grew concerned. I went back upstairs, wondering if she had lost sight of me and was waiting. I stepped aside with my large suitcase since the commuter traffic was so heavy. After about two minutes of not being able to find her, I called her phone. It went straight to voicemail. I called again, no answer. I then saw that she was calling me. I answered right away and said, "What happened? Where are you?"

GR managed to get out, "I'm in the eleva –" before the phone cut off.

This seemed very odd as she hated elevators, particularly when stairs or escalators were an option; she certainly would not choose to take an elevator without me. This fact, coupled with the abruptness with which the call ended, had me even more concerned. My mind started racing with fears that she had been abducted – a young single woman with luggage, looking like a tourist. I ran down to where the elevator opened and didn't see her on the platform.

None of this made sense; GR would never do this. We were literally just walking together, planning our trip back and talking about dinner. I started to panic. I couldn't get the thought of her being abducted out of my mind. When her phone kept going straight to voicemail, I called my sister Kate and told her what was happening. Could she see GR's location? Kate agreed that this was unusual behavior for GR, and when she couldn't track her phone she suggested I find the nearest police officer.

Kate remained on the phone with me as I ran up to an officer and explained what had happened.

"Sounds like she just took the elevator," he replied.

"No, you don't understand, this is my child, she wouldn't do this, she wouldn't leave me, and she rarely takes elevators."

He brought me into their offices, which were all glass and located right at the top of the platform. "How old is your daughter?" he asked, sharing a smirk with his fellow officer when I said twenty-one. He then told me she was an adult – as if I needed reminding of this! – and would be fine. Once again, and in a panicked voice, I pleaded with them to help me find her. They called her name over the loudspeaker, which could be heard throughout the entire San Pancras station.

"Grace-Rose, if you are in the station, please come to the top entry police offices."

They did this twice. I waited; still no sight of her. It had now been twelve minutes and I was starting to have trouble breathing. I stepped outside to see if perhaps I would get better cell service and be able to reach her. At this point, Kate was calling her too. I had never experienced a full-blown panic attack before and thought about the time GR called me from the nurse's office at school, thinking her lung had collapsed. I can't imagine how frightening that must have been.

Just as I had stepped outside, her name popped up on my phone.

"Are you okay?!" I gasped, "Where are you?"

"Yeah," she replied, "I'm waiting on the platform at the Northbound line. I had to take the elevator because my suitcase was too large. I saw you going down and just figured I would see you downstairs. I tried to tell you but my cell service cut out and I just jumped on the train to our transfer spot. I figured you had already gotten on and we'd meet at the next station."

She spoke as though this was completely normal behavior for her.

"But you left me!" I said, unable to believe she just got on the train without me. This wasn't the plan. This was something I had never experienced with her, especially with her previous, but now managed, anxiety.

As my heart stopped racing and my panic turned to sadness, I said, "Okay, you go ahead. I'll just meet you back at the house."

I then called my sister and, still in disbelief, filled her in. Kate, who was also a little surprised by GR's behavior, did her best to calm me down.

"She's okay," she said. "Let's just be relieved about that."

This was true. I started walking aimlessly with the large suitcase in tow, thinking to myself, *She's okay. She's okay.*

It hit me that this was a new, independent, confident, healthy, adult child of mine. I didn't know this child. She had been given these new life-saving pills. I had not. This was exactly what's supposed to happen but also something my mind had not been programmed for. This would be a huge psychological shift for me.

Cacio e Pepe with Panko Breadcrumbs

One of GR's favorite Italian dishes is cacio e pepe, we like to add panko or regular breadcrumbs. Il Pastaio in Beverly Hills serves a delicious cacio e pepe tableside directly from the parmesan wheel!

Ingredients

- Spaghetti or bucatini: 12 oz (about 3/4 of a standard package)
- Pecorino Romano cheese: 1 cup, finely grated
- Black pepper: 2 tsp, freshly cracked (adjust to taste)
- Butter: 2 tbsp
- Panko breadcrumbs: 1/2 cup
- Olive oil: 1 tbsp (for toasting breadcrumbs)
- Salt: for pasta water

Instructions

Step 1: Toast the Panko Breadcrumbs

1. In a small skillet, heat 1 tablespoon of olive oil over medium heat.
2. Add the panko breadcrumbs and stir frequently, toasting until golden brown (about 3–4 minutes). Remove from heat and set aside.

Step 2: Cook the Pasta

1. Bring a large pot of salted water to a boil and add the pasta. Cook until just *al dente* according to package instructions.
2. Reserve 1 cup of pasta water, then drain the pasta.

Step 3: Prepare the Cacio e Pepe Sauce

1. In a large skillet over medium heat, melt the butter and add the cracked black pepper. Let it cook for about 1 minute to release the pepper's aroma.

2. Add 1/2 cup of the reserved pasta water to the skillet, then add the drained pasta.

3. Reduce the heat to low. Gradually add the Pecorino Romano, tossing continuously to coat the pasta. Add more pasta water as needed until the cheese melts into a smooth, creamy sauce.

Step 4: Add the Panko and Serve

1. Once the pasta is well coated and creamy, taste and adjust pepper if desired.

2. Divide the pasta into bowls and top with the toasted panko breadcrumbs for crunch.

* For a little additional flavor, top with Lemon sea salt flakes.

TWENTY-FIVE

CHLA – FAREWELL TO CHILDHOOD

Children's hospitals are hard places to be. It's one thing to come in with a broken arm or cut that needs to be treated, but witnessing children with much more invasive conditions and diseases is truly heartbreaking. There's an entire oncology wing for small children battling cancer, a cruel diagnosis with the likely chance of the child never returning home.

What's more unusual is actually growing up in a children's hospital. Celebrating each birthday as a major milestone met with excitement and fear. Celebrating weight gain and growth but also watching pulmonary function decline with age. CF adult centers are relatively new concepts for the simple fact that people with CF weren't living to be adults.

We made it a routine to stop in the small chapel, which later became an entire non-denominational wing of the hospital. We would stop in and say a prayer and leave a small note for a child we had passed in the hospital that day. We would wish them well and simply be grateful to be going home. After some particularly challenging clinics, when test results were less than optimal, we'd stop by the Self-Realization Fellowship Center on Sunset Blvd near the hospital. I had learned about these centers, which were founded by Paramahansa Yogananda, after reading his book, *Autobiography of a Yogi*, when GR was young. The main one being on a lake in the Pacific Palisades, which recently, and miraculously, survived the Palisades fires.

They were incredibly peaceful and quiet. After hours in a small room, with a rotation of medical experts poking and prodding, asking a barrage of questions, and reviewing test or lab results, GR and I would both be exhausted. Going to their small meditation shrine and sitting in silence beneath the trees, allowed us to step away from the noise for a while.

Not wanting clinic days to trigger only bad memories, I also always made a point of doing a little something fun afterward. Sometimes, we would stop at Figaro, a little French cafe on Vermont Ave., for cheese fondue or an eclair. Other times, we'd pop into a nearby vintage store and play dress-up. Anything to make us feel a little normal again. I once read that "the only way of feeling normalcy is to ignore the weight of reality," and during these times it felt accurate.

After thirty years in practice, GR's pulmonary doctor had recently retired. I believe he felt confident in the direction this disease was headed. He'd often tell us, "This is a great time to have CF." As oxymoronic as that sounded, the truth was with the advancements in medicine and research, it was likely that as long as she stayed well enough to be a recipient of these medications, she may live a longer, healthier life.

We still had one CF clinic at children's hospital left. GR could have chosen to leave and enter an adult center when she turned eighteen, but she chose to stay at CHLA, which they would allow until she turned twenty-one. Her reasoning was that she'd rather be walking into a hospital with aquariums, storytelling circles, and gift shops with toys rather than an adult hospital. The few times she had been to adult hospitals, she felt as though everything was monotonous, serious, and somewhat depressing. I wouldn't be surprised if parents of younger kids in the clinic questioned seeing this tall, young adult among the patients. Her feet used to dangle off the bed in the clinic room, now they reached the floor.

Since GR was abroad when she turned twenty-one, her medical team had agreed to see her for her final clinic when she returned. Actually, it was more of a farewell than a proper visit, with them giving her options for adult centers, along with navigating insurance and pharmacies. We brought the team souvenirs from London, and they had all signed sweet notes inside of a copy of Dr. Seuss's, *Oh the Places You'll Go.*

It's unusual to say you grew up in a hospital. One foot in each door, you learn empathy on another level.

Walking into this final visit was very emotional for me – realizing that we were leaving for good, that GR was officially an adult. But, also, incredibly grateful that she's *an adult.*

We want to dedicate this chapter to CHLA and the team that took such great care of her.

Eternal Gratitude.

Street Corn (Elotes)

We first had this corn at Cafe Habana on Prince Street in New York when GR was four years old. She fell in love with it and was excited when they later opened a location in Malibu. We also found it at the farmers market that CHLA had in one of the courtyards on Wednesdays. We usually had clinic days on Wednesday, so the corn became a treat to look forward to afterward.

Ingredients:

- 4 ears of corn, husked
- 1/4 cup mayonnaise
- 1/4 cup sour cream (or Mexican crema, if available)
- 1/2 cup Cotija cheese, crumbled (feta works as a substitute if needed)
- 1 tablespoon fresh lime juice
- 1 teaspoon tajin (adjust to taste)
- Salt and pepper, to taste
- Fresh cilantro, chopped (optional garnish)
- Lime wedges, for serving

Instructions:

1. Grill the Corn:

   Preheat your grill to medium-high heat. Place the corn directly on the grill grates, turning occasionally, until it's nicely charred in spots (about 7-10 minutes). Alternatively, you can use a stovetop grill pan or even roast the corn in a 400°F oven until it's cooked and slightly browned.

2. Prepare the Sauce:

   In a small bowl, mix together the mayonnaise, sour cream (or crema), lime juice, salt, and pepper.

3. Coat the Corn:

   Once the corn is cooked, brush or spread the mayo mixture evenly over each ear of corn. Sprinkle tajin and crumbled Cotija cheese generously over the top.

4. Garnish and Serve:

   Garnish with chopped cilantro if you like and serve with lime wedges on the side.

Best served as a side to fish tacos.

* Tajin is a spicy Mexican salt - it's also frequently served on top of fruits

EPILOGUE

As I write this, Grace-Rose's graduation from NYU Tisch Film & TV Production is just a few months away, in May 2025. It has been an incredible journey getting here, and my pride and gratitude cannot be put into words. She is currently working on her senior thesis – a short film about her absentee father called *Long Time, No See*.

I love reading her stories and ideas, one of her most recent being a treatment for a screenwriting class prompt about "dark comedy." She had relived this moment, titled it "5 Wishes," and pitched it with comedic relief.

When the Professor asked her what inspired this, she wrote…

"Fun fact: I used to be terminally ill, but let's brush over that.

Just before my eighteenth birthday I was given a booklet from my doctors regarding my 'wishes' in the event I was too ill or too dead to speak on my own behalf. The idea was to legally let them know who was in charge of pulling the plug, and how I'd want to go whether I be buried, cremated, etc. After the initial panic attack, I redirected that energy into creating a dark comedy/coming-of-age short film. I think this would be an interesting way to represent the terminally ill without the premise being a romance between them and another terminally ill patient."

When I read the part about her saying, "I used to be terminally ill," my eyes filled with tears. "Used to be" was ringing in my head.

Reading those words, I couldn't help but think that death is inevitable; it's the weight of life itself that is so heavy. A weight I'm happy to carry with her...

"Per Aspera, Ad Astra"
(Through Adversity to the Stars)

AFTERWORD

GR was given the choice of three images to write a short story about for her NYU application.

She chose an image of a little girl about the age she was when Hurricane Katrina hit. This is what she wrote.

It was adapted from the book, "Silly Sally," that we read endlessly throughout the drive referred to in chapter four of this book.

The Memories A Birthday May Bring

The off-pitch chorus of my family's singing fades out. I lean in, take a deep breath, and make a wish. The smell of buttercream frosting becomes overpowered by the smoke from eighteen candles. I've heard scent has a stronger link to memory and emotion than any of the other senses. It brings me back to the day we left New Orleans and the smell of fried powerlines. It had been five days since Hurricane Katrina hit. The winds tore down power lines and the Bayou had become one with the streets. Since it was cooler outside than in our home, we slept on the balcony. I was two and three-quarters, sitting outside cradling my baby doll. The dark apartment was hotter than the humid summer heat outside. The windows were open but the curtains remained still.

That one moment, that small whiff of smoke brought me back to
the move and the unknown of where we'd end up.

Like clowns in a car; me, my grandmother, aunt, mom, cat, and
fish.

First stop, Texas, with 348 miles to go. I had one book on the trip,
Silly Sally, and so we began reading…

"Silly Sally went to town, walking backwards, upside down. On the
way she met a pig, a silly pig, they danced a jig."

Houston was packed with those displaced from the storm. I
remember staying one night to rest from the road but not much longer.
My poor fish went from a plastic bag to hotel coffee pots along the
way. Next stop, San Antonio, with 189 miles to go and so we continued reading…

"Silly Sally went to town, walking backwards, upside down. On the
way she met a dog, a silly dog, they played leapfrog."

One step into that hotel room and we woke up to an army of
crickets; you can imagine our cat was having the time of her life. We
didn't stay long. Next stop Phoenix, with 982 miles to go; we continued reading…

"Silly Sally went to town, leaping backwards, upside down. On the
way she met a loon, a silly loon, they sang a tune."

Apparently, that was the first night my mom had service to get
ahold of her messages. I don't remember much about this night but
I remember the pancakes I was promised the next morning and they
did not disappoint. We had two options for the next morning. Behind
door number one was to continue further west to visit family. The first
look at a family member's newborn and a city holding the memories
of my mom's twenties. Behind door number two, the long haul back
but with nowhere to go. No guaranteed roof, water, or electricity, so
further west we drove. Next stop, Los Angeles, with 337 miles to go;
we continued reading…

"Silly Sally went to town, singing backwards, upside down. On the
way she met a sheep, a silly sheep, they fell asleep."

After five days of staying with my mom's eldest sister, a pamphlet to an open unit available was heavily suggested. Coming up quickly were the holidays, the first one away from home, starting off strong with my third birthday. I remember celebrating in a park nearby our apartment as my mom captured moments on her new camera. I snap out of it as the sound of applause and cheers crescendo back in. My mother sets the birthday box, decorated with glitter glue and macaroni, on the table beside me.

I'm an adult... legally not mentally. As I remove these candles, the smell of buttercream returns and fixes the inner child. I place the candles inside the box along with the rest of the wax numbers. Scattered in the box are some pictures from previous birthdays. I gently pick up the eldest one to date from November 27, 2005. The image captured me on my third birthday wandering through the park where we first celebrated in the city that became home.

Crawfish Étouffée

In Louisiana, we often use the term a little lagniappe (LAN-yap), which is Cajun-French for something given gratuitously or by way of good measure. This extra recipe, a Louisiana favorite, is a little lagniappe for taking this journey with us.

Servings: 4-6
Prep Time: 15 minutes
Cook Time: 40 minutes

Ingredients

- 1/2 cup (1 stick) unsalted butter
- 1/2 cup all-purpose flour
- 1 medium onion, finely chopped
- 1 green bell pepper, finely chopped
- 2 stalks celery, finely chopped
- 4 cloves garlic, minced
- 2 cups seafood or chicken stock (preferably homemade or low-sodium)
- 1 (10-ounce) can diced tomatoes (optional, for a tomato-based variation)
- 2 teaspoons Cajun or Creole seasoning
- 1/2 teaspoon smoked paprika
- 1/4 teaspoon cayenne pepper (adjust to heat preference)
- 1 teaspoon dried thyme
- 1 teaspoon Worcestershire sauce
- 1 lb cooked crawfish tails, peeled and deveined (with fat if available)
- 2 green onions, thinly sliced (for garnish)
- 2 tablespoons fresh parsley, chopped (for garnish)
- Salt and black pepper, to taste

- Steamed white rice, for serving
- Hot sauce (optional, for extra heat)

Instructions

1. **Make the Roux:**
   - In a large skillet or Dutch oven, melt the butter over medium heat. Gradually whisk in the flour, stirring constantly, to make a roux. Cook until it reaches a light caramel or peanut butter color (about 8-10 minutes), stirring frequently to prevent burning.

2. **Sauté the Vegetables:**
   - Add the onions, bell pepper, and celery to the roux. Cook for 5-7 minutes, stirring, until the vegetables are soft and translucent. Add the garlic and cook for 1 minute until fragrant.

3. **Build the Flavor:**
   - Slowly stir in the seafood or chicken stock, a little at a time, until fully incorporated and smooth. If using, stir in the diced tomatoes. Add the Cajun seasoning, smoked paprika, cayenne pepper, thyme, and Worcestershire sauce. Simmer the mixture on low heat for 15-20 minutes, stirring occasionally.

4. **Add the Crawfish:**
   - Gently stir in the crawfish tails. Cook for 5-7 minutes, or until the crawfish are heated through. Taste and adjust seasoning with salt, pepper, or more Cajun seasoning if needed.

5. **Serve:**
   - Ladle the Crawfish Étouffée over steamed white rice. Garnish with green onions, parsley, and a splash of hot sauce if desired.

And, as always, Just Add Salt.

ACKNOWLEDGMENTS

"It takes a village to raise a child" is an African proverb expressing the collectivist understanding that the entire community – not just one individual or organization – is responsible for a child's development. Indeed, it reflects the values of traditional African cultures, where the entire community was involved in the raising of children.

My village spans far and wide. My gratitude, even further.

To my immediate family – Grace (Mom), Tom (Dad), Allison (sister), Mac (brother), Kate (sister), Mark (brother-in-law), JohnMichael (brother-in-law), Grace-Rose (you know by now), Zander (nephew), Jasper (nephew), Coco (niece), and Dean (uncle).

To my extended family – my aunts, uncles, and many cousins. To my "chosen family" and my closest friends, you absolutely know who you are.

To my friends in the cities I call home – New Orleans, Los Angeles, and New York. I appreciate you all immensely. It would require a whole new book to name everyone. I truly feel blessed!

To my London swap-mate who allowed me the serene environment in which I was able to write (and later finish) this book.

To my dear L.A. friend who gave me a home when I wasn't sure where that was anymore...

To CHAOS for guiding me to the cosmos.

To my editor – Thank you for your encouragement and guidance.

To my publisher – For steering the ship!

To the volunteers – Every person who ever volunteered, donated, acquired, or gave auction items, participated, and simply showed up for us (some of you, repeatedly for years). I will always remember your generosity.

To the doctors, nurses, social workers, and every other member of GR's medical team(s). Without you, we quite literally wouldn't be here.

To the fundraisers and donors – We are incredibly grateful for your support.

To the medical researchers – Your tireless efforts will never go unnoticed.

To Vertex pharmaceuticals – for developing life-saving drugs.

To the Make-A-Wish Foundation – Thank you for granting GR's wish and letting her remain involved.

To Children's Hospital Los Angeles (the staff, medical team, and corporate members) – we see you and we appreciate you.

To the CF California Winemasters – For making us feel incredibly special and hopeful year after year with your relentless work and dedication to this cause. GR's exclamation said it best: "Thank YOU!"

To the Cystic Fibrosis Foundation – You have changed the trajectory of this disease and prolonged lives, which is nothing short of miraculous.

Thank you all.

RECOMMENDED CYSTIC FIBROSIS BOOKS

Breath from Salt: A Deadly Genetic Disease, a New Era in Science, and the Patients and Families Who Changed Medicine Forever (Bijal P. Trivedi)

Salt in My Soul: An Unfinished Life (Mallory Smith)

Exhale: Hope, Healing, and a Life in Transplant (David Weill, M.D.)

Little Matches: A Memoir of Finding Light in the Dark (Maryann O'Hara)

CF Warrior Project (Andy Lipman)

Beyond Breathing (Margarete Cassalina)

Alex, Life of a child (Frank deFord)

Ten percent of all book sales from *Just Add Salt* benefit
The Grace Rose Foundation.

ABOUT THE AUTHOR

Born and raised in the vibrant cultural hub of New Orleans, Leah's journey has been one of resilience, creativity, and purpose. After attending the Fashion Institute of Technology (FIT) in New York City, she moved to Hong Kong to work and immerse herself in the international fashion industry. Later, she moved to Los Angeles to establish her own clothing company, bringing her distinctive design vision to life.

Leah's entrepreneurial spirit enabled her to launch retail stores, carrying her designs, in New Orleans and Los Angeles. The move back to her hometown and the birth of her daughter took a dramatic turn following Hurricane Katrina. Evacuating with her two-year old, who was born with Cystic Fibrosis, Leah relocated to Los Angeles for access to specialized medical care. She continued to grow her design business while embarking on a mission to raise awareness and funds for Cystic Fibrosis research.

Together with her daughter, Grace-Rose, Leah co-founded the clothing line *Rosie G*, a project that combined their shared creativity with a passion for advocacy. They also established a non-profit foundation, *The Grace Rose Foundation*, dedicated to raising awareness about Cystic Fibrosis and championing mental health initiatives for youth.

Most recently, Leah has added author to her endeavors, having written a memoir that chronicles her inspiring journey of determination, artistry, and advocacy. Looking ahead, she is excited to expand her creative ventures and passion for storytelling, continuing to enrich her community and inspire others.

Stay in Touch:

JustAddSaltBook.com
Book Instagram - @justaddsaltbook
Author Instagram - @leahmilana